Thicket Priory
A History

Bruce Corrie and
Colin Blanshard Withers
2022

Published by the Authors

First Edition
2022

Unless otherwise indicated, all materials on these pages are the copyright of Bruce Corrie. All rights reserved. No part of these pages, either text or image, may be used for any purpose other than personal use. Therefore, reproduction, modification, storage in a retrieval system or retransmission, in any form or by any means—electronic, mechanical or otherwise—for reasons other than personal use, is strictly prohibited without prior written permission.

While the authors believe that the information given in this work is correct, readers must rely upon their own skill and judgement when making use of it. The authors assume no liability to anyone for any loss or damage caused by any error or omission in the work, whether the error or omission is the result of negligence or any other cause.

The authors accept no responsibility for the continued existence of URLs pointing to third party internet websites referred to in this work, nor that any content on those websites are relevant or accurate.

Published by Thicket Priory Publishing

Copyright © Bruce Corrie, 2022

ISBN 978-1-7393344-3-7

All rights reserved. No part of this publication may be reproduced, stored in a retrieval system or transmitted in any form or by any means, electronic, mechanical, photocopying, recording or otherwise, without the prior written permission of the publishers.

Printed in Great Britain

PREFACE

The history of Thicket Priory is quite unusual. The original priory was in existence by 1180, and founded possibly as early as 1162. When Henry VIII broke from the Catholic Church to form the Church of England, a process that began in 1529 and was completed by 1537, most of the abbeys, monasteries and priories that were then demolished during the infamous Dissolution of the Monasteries were not rebuilt. However, Thicket Priory was one of the very few exceptions, and was rebuilt not once, but more than once.

The complete story of the various incarnations of Thicket Priory, its original sisterhood and its subsequent owners, is contained in three booklets, which are fully referenced and annotated. They are: *Thicket Priory: Foundation to Dissolution*; *Thicket Priory: Dissolution to Thicket Priory II*; and *Thicket Priory: Rebirth and the Return of the Nuns*.

This book combines the text of the three booklets in the series, but in a less academic and more narrative style, and includes a number of photographs, maps and plans, scans of historical documents, coats of arms and illustrations to give a fuller appreciation of the priory.

ACKNOWLEDGEMENTS

Our grateful thanks are due to the archivists and staff of The National Archives (TNA), who have been unstinting in their support and suggestions, and to Bruce Westcott and Dr. Matthew Tompkins of Leicester University for their help with the more tricky idiosyncrasies of medieval Latin and administrative practice.

Thanks are also due to the staff of the Borthwick Institute for Archives at the University of York, for their help with the medieval registers of the archbishops of York; the staff of the Department of Manuscripts in the British Library; and all the staff of the various archives and libraries throughout Yorkshire who helped in locating and providing digital copies of many unpublished manuscripts.

Last but not least, our thanks must also go to the last remaining member of the Dunnington-Jefferson family who once lived at Thicket Priory, Rosemary Nicolette Dunnington-Jefferson (Nicky to her friends), who proof-read the entire text and provided many corrections and observations.

CONTENTS

Sources and Abbreviations — vi
Select Bibliography – Archbishops' Registers – Abbreviations

Chapter 1 – Foundation of Thicket Priory I to the Dissolution — 1
The Benedictines – Foundation of Thicket Priory – The Construction of the Priory
Economy of the Priory – Internal Community – External Community – Dissolution

Chapter 2 – Dissolution to Thicket Priory II — 45
The Aftermath of the Dissolution – The Aske Family – The Robinson Family
The Jefferson Family – The Dunnington Family – Change of Name
Thicket and Ellerton Estate Buildings

Chapter 3 – Thicket Priory II to Thicket Priory III — 71
The Building of Thicket Priory III – Sad News - Victorian Life at the Priory
Joseph John Dunnington-Jefferson – Tragic Event – Thicket Priory III for Rent

Chapter 4 – Estate Management — 81
William Burland – Letter-Books – Reginald Pearce-Brown – Andrew Moscrop
James Eric Smith – Colin Bell

Chapter 5 – WWI and the Inter-War Years — 87
John Alexander Dunnington-Jefferson – Wilfrid Mervyn Dunnington-Jefferson
Ella Dunnington-Jefferson – WWI Roll of Honour – The Inter-War Years

Chapter 6 – WWII and the Post-War Years — 93
Lieutenant Colonel John Alexander Dunnington-Jefferson
Social Changes – The Return of the Nuns
Subsequent Ownership and Thicket Priory IV

Epilogue — 101

Sources and Abbreviations

Select Bibliography

ALLISON, K. J., (ed.), *A History of the County of York, East Riding*: vol. 3, *Ouse and Derwent Wapentake, and Part of Harthill Wapentake*, (London, 1976)

BAILDON, William Paley, *Notes on the Religious and Secular Houses of Yorkshire*, 2 volumes, YASRS 17 and 81 (1895, 1931)

BURTON, Janet, *The Yorkshire Nunneries in the Twelfth and Thirteenth Centuries*, Borthwick Papers 56, (York: Borthwick Institute of Historical Research, 1979)

BURTON, John, *Monasticon Eboracense and the Ecclesiastical History of Yorkshire*, (York, 1758)

BURTON, Thomas, (original author), RAINE, James, (edited and enlarged by), *The History and Antiquities of the Parish of Hemingbrough in the County of York*, (York, 1888)

CARPENTER, David X., *The Cartulary of St. Leonard's Hospital, York*, 2 vol. set: YASRS vol. CLXIII, and BTS, 42, (2015)

CLAY, Charles and GREENWAY, Diana E., *Early Yorkshire Families* (Cambridge University Press, 2013)

DUGDALE, Sir William, (A New Edition by Caley, Ellis and Bandinel), *Monasticon Anglicanum*, 6 vols., (1846–1849)

FARRER, William (first 3 vols.), CLAY, Charles Travis (vols. 4–12), *Early Yorkshire Charters*, 12 vols., (1914–1965)

FOSTER, Joseph, (ed.), *The visitation of Yorkshire, made in the years 1584–85: to which is added the subsequent visitation made in 1612, by Richard St. George, Norry King of Arms*, Privately Printed, (London, 1875)

FOWLER, J. T., (ed.), *Memorials of the Abbey of St. Mary of Fountains, vol. III, Bursars' Books, 1456–1459, and Memorandum Book of Thomas Swynton, 1446–1458*, Surtees Society vol. CXXX, (1918)

JAMES, Mervyn, *Society, Politics and Culture: Studies in Early Modern England*, (Cambridge University Press, 1986)

KNOWLES, David; SMITH, David M., *The Heads of Religious Houses: England and Wales*, III. 1377–1540 (London, 2011)

LANCASTER, William T., *Abstracts of the charters and other documents contained in the chartulary of the Cistercian Abbey of Fountains in the West Riding of the County of York*, 2 vols., (1915)

PAGE, William, (ed.), *A History of the County of York*, vol. III, *Religious Houses*, (London, 1974)

PURVIS, J. S., (ed.), 'A Selection of Monastic Rentals and Dissolution Papers', in *Miscellanea III*, YASRS 80, (1931)

RAINE, James, (ed.), *Testamenta Eboracensia*, Surtees Society, vols. 4, 30, 45, 53, (London, 1836–1869)

RECORD COMMISSIONERS, *Valor Ecclesiasticus, Temp. Henr. VIII, Auctoritate Regia, Institutus*, vol. 5, Diocese of York, Chester, Carlisle, Durham, (1826)

SKAIFE, Robert H., *The Register of the Guild of Corpus Christi in the City of York*, Surtees Society, vol. LVII, (London, 1871)

WAITES, Brian, 'The Monasteries of North-East Yorkshire and the Medieval Wool Trade', in *Yorkshire Archaeological Journal*, vol. 52, (1980)

WITHERS, Colin Blanshard, *Thicket Priory: Foundation to Dissolution*, (2022)

WITHERS, Colin Blanshard, *Thicket Priory: Dissolution to Thicket Priory II*, (2022)

WITHERS, Colin Blanshard, *Thicket Priory: Rebirth and the Return of the Nuns*, (2022)

WOODWARD, G. W. O., 'The Exemption from Suppression of Certain Yorkshire Priories', in *The English Historical Review*, no. CCC, (July 1961)

Archbishops' Registers

Reg.Corbridge	BROWN, William, (ed.), *The Register of Thomas of Corbridge: Lord Archbishop of York 1300–1304*, 2 vols., Surtees Society, vols. 138, 141, (1925–1928)
Reg.Greenfield	BROWN, William, (ed.), *The Register of William Greenfield, Lord Archbishop of York, 1306–1315*, 5 vols., Surtees Society, vols. 145, 149, 151, 152, 153, (1931–1940)
Reg.Romeyn	BROWN, William, (ed.), *The Register of John Le Romeyn, Lord Archbishop of York, 1286–1296*, 2 vols., Surtees Society, vols. 123, 128, (1913–1917)
Reg.Rotherham	BARKER, E. E., (ed.), *The Register of Thomas Rotherham, Archbishop of York, 1480–1500*, vol. 1, Canterbury and York Society, vol. 69, (1976)
Reg.Melton	HILL, ROBINSON, BROCKLESBY, TIMMINS, (eds.), *The Register of William Melton, Archbishop of York, 1317–1340*, 6 vols., Canterbury and York Society, vols. 70, 71, 76, 85, 93, 101, (1977–2011)

Reg.Scrope   SWANSON, R. N., (ed.), *A Calendar of the Register of Richard Scrope, Archbishop of York, 1397*, 2 vols., BTC 8, 11, (1981–1985)

Reg.Waldby   SMITH, D. M., (ed.), *A Calendar of the Register of Robert Waldby, Archbishop of York, 1397*, BTC 2, (1974)

Abbreviations

BI   The Borthwick Institute for Archives, University of York

CCR   Calendar of the Close Rolls

CFR   *Calendar of Fine Rolls preserved in the Public Record Office.* (London: HMSO, 1911–1962)

CIM   *Calendar of Inquisitions Miscellaneous (Chancery) preserved in the Public Record Office.* (London: HMSO, 1916–present)

CIPM   *Calendar of Inquisitions Post-Mortem and other Analogous Documents preserved in the Public Record Office.* (London: HMSO, 1904–present)

CPR   *Calendar of the Patent Rolls preserved in the Public Record Office.* (London: HMSO, 1891–1986)

EYC   Early Yorkshire Charters

EYF   Early Yorkshire Families

L&P   Letters and Papers, Foreign and Domestic, of the Reign of Henry VIII

HMSO   His/Her Majesty's Stationery Office

TNA   The National Archives, Kew, London

VCH   Victoria County History

YAJ   Yorkshire Archaeological Journal

YASRS   Yorkshire Archaeological Society, Record Series

CHAPTER 1
Foundation of Thicket Priory I to the Dissolution

The Benedictines - Foundation of Thicket Priory - The Construction of the Priory
Economy of the Priory - Internal Community - External Community - Dissolution

The Benedictines

Benedict of Nursia (A.D. 480–547) studied in Rome from an early age, but was so disillusioned by the immorality he found there that at the age of fourteen he gave up his studies and lived an hermitic life in a cave in Subiaco around fifty miles east of Rome. His great piety attracted followers and he founded several communities for monks near Rome, before establishing an abbey at Monte Cassino in the mountains of southern Italy.

While at the abbey he wrote his famous Rule, which set out in seventy-three simple chapters his principles for leading a monastic life. The Rule covered: how to live a Christocentric life; how to administer a monastery efficiently; how to behave obediently and humbly (and what to do with inmates who were refractory); how to manage the work of God (the *Opus Dei* of the Catholic Church); and the management of a monastery.

Benedict was influenced in writing his Rule by the works of the monk Johan Cassian (John the Ascetic) and by the *Regula Magistri* (Rule of the Master), but was more reasonable and balanced, making it attractive to Christian communities, and its popularity spread. Around A.D. 594 Pope Gregory the Great praised the Rule, and Benedict, which further increased the popularity of both. Communities of Benedictines sprang up rapidly throughout Europe, and in A.D. 816/17 an important synod declared that Benedict's Rule was binding for all monks.

Saint Benedict

Scholastica (c. 480–1543) was the sister of Benedict of Nursia, and according to one tradition was the twin sister of Benedict. Scholastica established a community of consecrated virgins close to Monte Cassino which has been traditionally considered the first convent of Benedictine nuns.

The Benedictines were never an 'order' in the normal sense of the word. Rather, it was a loose confederation of independent religious houses. They were typically governed by an abbot or prior (abbess or prioress), and modelled on the 'family', with the abbot or prior being the 'father' and the monks 'brothers', and similarly the abbess or prioress being the 'mother' and the nuns 'sisters'. They were easily distinguished from other monks due to their black habits, which led them to be called the Black Monks.

In England, Augustine of Canterbury and his monks established the first English Benedictine monastery at Canterbury soon after their arrival in the late sixth century, and the Benedictine Rule spread rapidly. In the north of England it was adopted in most of the monasteries that had been founded by the Celtic missionaries, beginning with Whitby in A.D. 657.

Saint Scholastica

However, all the monasteries in the north were destroyed during the Danish invasions of the ninth and tenth centuries, and this desolation continued until the Danes were

1

themselves supplanted by the Normans following the Conquest. Janet Burton wrote: 'Yorkshire in 1066 could truly be called a "monastic wilderness"; indeed apart from a few quasi-religious settlements such as that which may have existed at the church of Holy Trinity, York, there was a complete absence of recognizable monastic life north of the river Trent'.

Following the establishment of Selby Abbey in 1069, and Whitby c. 1078, the Benedictines once again began to flourish. By 1140 the number of religious houses in Yorkshire rose to around twenty, and included two, possibly three, nunneries. In the second half of the twelfth century twelve more monasteries were founded, but over twenty nunneries. Unfortunately, the chronology of the foundation of these early nunneries is problematic due to a lack of documentary evidence, and only one nunnery, that of Nunkeeling, is known to have had a cartulary.

The Benedictine nunneries established in Yorkshire in the thirteenth century and early fourteenth century, with approximate dates of foundation, were: York, St. Clement's, (1125x1133); Nunkeeling, (1143x1153); Wilberfoss, (1147x1153); Nun Monkton, (1147x1153); Arden, (1147x1169); Marrick, (1154x1158); Yedingham, (*ante* 1158); Thicket, (*ante* 1180); Nunburnholme, (*ante* 1188); Foukeholme, (*ante* 1226, dissolved 1308–12).

At this point it is necessary, for reasons that will be made clear in the External Community section, briefly to discuss the Cistercian Order.

The name Cistercian is derived from Cistercium (the Latin for Cîteaux, near Dijon) in eastern France, where the Order branched off from the Benedictines in 1098 after a group of monks from Molesme founded Cîteaux Abbey.

The Cistercians still followed the Rule of Benedict, but rejected the developments the Benedictines had undergone, and tried to go back to the Rule as it had been during Saint Benedict's lifetime. They were readily distinguishable from the original Benedictines due to their undyed woollen habits, which led them to be called the White Monks.

The Order grew in popularity and by the end of the twelfth century had spread throughout Europe, reaching England in 1128, when Waverley Abbey was founded in Surrey. In Yorkshire, Rievaulx Abbey was founded in 1131, Fountains Abbey in 1132 and Meaux in 1151.

The Cistercians employed their own manual labour to obtain self-sufficiency. They accepted gifts of land on which to build their houses, farm sheep for wool and grow food, quarry stone and retrieve timber for building and repairs. However, initially at least, they would accept only undeveloped land.

In 1132, in return for the support of the Cistercians during the Great Schism, Pope Innocent II, granted the Order freedom from the paying of tithes from land they cultivated themselves. This led to some Benedictine nunneries claiming to be Cistercian simply to avoid paying tithes, and the abbot of Cîteaux complained directly about this practice.

Foundation of Thicket Priory

Before the foundation of Thicket Priory is discussed certain clarifications need to be made concerning the persons mentioned. It has been held that the founder of Thicket Priory was Roger son of Roger, and that this man was in fact Roger Hay. The origin of this identification was *Early Yorkshire Charters, vol. ii*, by Farrer, and *Early Yorkshire Families*, by Clay and Greenway. Farrer provided the following:

'Robert Fossard apparently enfeoffed Roger, father of Roger, of these 6 carucates [manor of Aughton], 4 in Everthorpe, 4 in North Cave, and 6 in Goodmanham to hold for the service of one knight. This was one of the 2 fees held in 1166 by Roger, son of Roger. He was succeeded by Thomas Hay, apparently his son and heir, and presumably husband of Emma Hay, daughter of Roger, son of Alured. Thomas Hay I confirmed a gift made to the hospital of St. Peter, York, by the younger Roger, his father-in-law, as given above.'

The use of 'apparently' and 'presumably' show that Farrer was being cautious in the absence of proof. However, Clay and Greenway, summarising and expanding Farrer, removed the caution, and stated the following as fact:

'In 1166 Roger son of Roger held 2 knights' fees of William Fossard, consisting of land in Huggate, North Cave, Everthorpe (par. N. Cave), Aughton and Laytham (par. Aughton). He was the founder of Thicket Priory, and was succeeded by his son Thomas, who confirmed gifts in North Cave made by his father Roger *Hay* [my italics] to St. Peter's hospital, c. 1175–1188. Thomas married Emma daughter and heir of Roger son of Alvred, and died before Michaelmas 1190, when Thomas son of Thomas son of Roger paid 100s. for a recognition of the death of his father respecting land in Aughton and Goodmanham, of which Roger de Hay was deforcing him.' A note on this text states that the last named Roger de Hay 'has not been identified; he may have been a younger brother of Thomas the elder.'

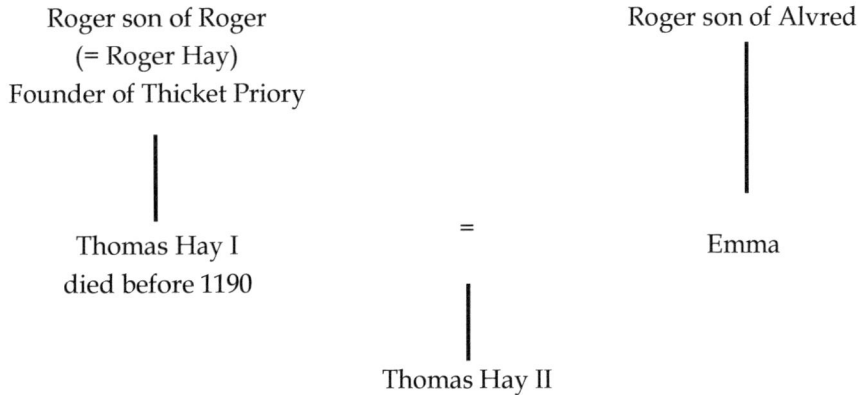

It was Carpenter who demonstrated that the above pedigree was in error on several points, and Farrer had been right to be cautious. Roger son of Roger was not identical with Roger Hay. Roger son of Roger did not have a son named Thomas, and, in fact, died without issue, and Emma did not marry Thomas Hay, but was sister to Roger and Thomas, sons of Roger, and married the Roger de Hay that Clay and Greenway were unable to identify.

Revised Pedigree of the Founders of Thicket Priory

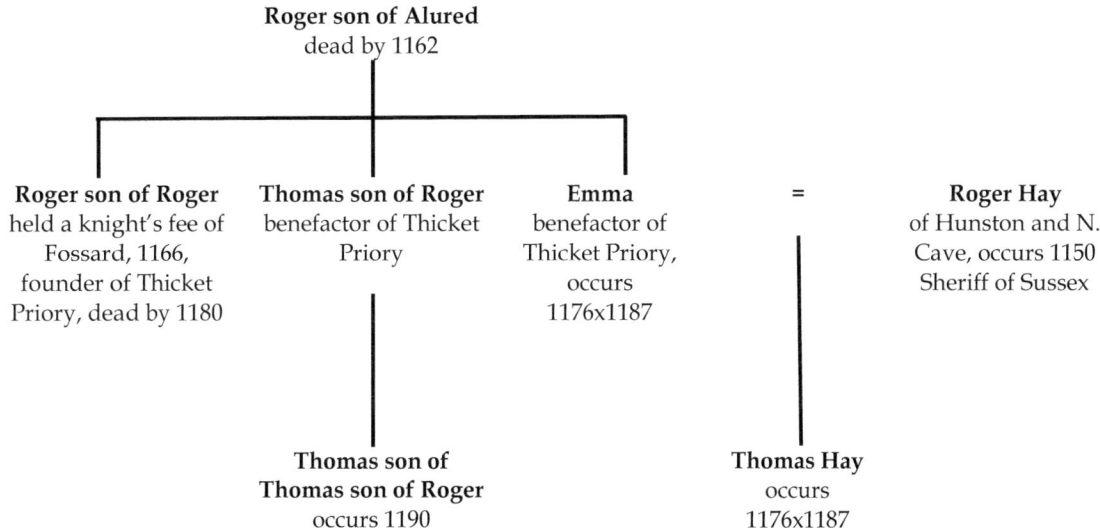

Roger de Hay of North Cave was identical with Roger de Hay of Hunston (near Chichester) and sheriff of Sussex 1163–1170. He lived mainly on his Sussex estates, explaining why he left little mark in Yorkshire, and died between 1190 and 1196. Carpenter also showed that Emma was the daughter of Roger, son of Alured, but crucially the heir of her brother, Roger, son of Roger. Carpenter corrected these errors and provided a pedigree. The following notes on the foundation and endowments of Thicket Priory should therefore be used with reference to the above revised pedigree.

We know that Thicket was in existence during the reign of Richard I, and was founded during the reign of Henry II, as one of the original benefactors had died before 1180. A confirmation charter of King John exists, dated 27 February, in the fifth year of his reign, (1203–4), which lists the first seven benefactors:

Carta Regis Johannis
[Cart. 5 Johannis, m. 12, n. 98. Pat. 13 Edw. I. m. 20.]

> *Johannes Dei gratia, &c. Sciatis nos intuitu Dei et pro salute animæ nostræ et animarum antecessorum et successorum concessisse et præsenti carta nostra confirmasse Deo et ecclesiæ sanctæ Mariæ de Thikeheved et monialibus Ibidem Deo servientibus rationabiles donationes eis factas inferius scriptas; scilicet de dono Rogeri fil. Rogeri locum qui dicitur Tikeheved et iiij. bovatas terræ cum pertinentiis in Cottungwich. De dono Thomæ fil. Rogeri dimid. carucatam terræ cum pertinen. in eadem villa. De dono Picot unam bovatam terræ cum pertinentiis in eadem villa. De dono et concessione Gaufridi de Ficelingham et Hugonis de Buleton essartum quoddam de wasto nostro. De dono Rogeri filii Rogeri unam bovatam terræ cum pertinentiis in Gudemundeham. De dono Emmæ sororis ejusdem Rogeri filii Rogeri unam bovatam terræ cum pertinentiis in eadem villa. De dono Gaufridi de Ficelingham duas bovatas terræ cum pertinentiis in Coldric. De dono Hugonis de Boulton duas bovatas terræ cum pertinentiis in eadem villa. De dono Emmæ de Diholton unam bovatam terræ cum pertimentiis in eadem villa. Quare volo, &c. Testibus domino G. archiepiscopo Eborac. Ph. Dunelm. episcopo. G. fil. Petri, &c. Rob. filio Rogeri. Hugone de Nevill. Datum per manum S. præpositi Beverlaci et Wellensis archidiaconi, apud Eboracum, vicesimo septimo die Februarii, anno, &c. quinto.*

John by the grace of God, etc. Know that in consideration of God and for the salvation of our soul and that of our ancestors and successors and by our charter at hand have confirmed to God and the church of St. Mary Thickhead and the nuns serving God in the same place the grants [in due form] made as written below; namely of the gift of Roger son of Roger the place called Thickhead and four oxgangs of land with the appurtenances belonging in Cottingwith. The gift of Thomas son of Roger half a carucate of land with the appurtenances belonging in the same township. The gift of Picot one oxgang of land with the appurtenances belonging in the same township. The gift and grant of Geoffrey of Ficelingham [Fitling] and Hugh of Bolton essart of land of our [the king's] waste. The gift of Roger son of Roger one oxgang of land with the appurtenances belonging in Goodmanham. The gift of Emma sister of the same Roger son of Roger, one oxgang of land with the appurtenances belonging in the same township. The gift of Geoffrey of Ficelingham two oxgangs of land with the appurtenances belonging in Queldrick [Wheldrake]. The gift of Hugh of Bolton two oxgangs of land with the appurtenances belonging in the same township. The gift of Emma of Diholton one oxgang of land with the appurtenances belonging in the same township. Why I, etc. Witnesses: lord Geoffrey Archbishop of York; Philip, Bishop of Durham; G. son of Peter, etc; Robert son of Roger; Hugh de Nevill. Given by hand, Simon, provost of Beverley and archdeacon of Wells, at York.

This confirmation charter gives no clue as to the dates of the original grants, but the founder's grant was before 1180, and one later charter refers to a grant made during the reign of Richard I, 1189x1199. Another charter gives a clue as to the identity of possibly the first prioress of Thicket, Sibilla. These later charters were printed in their original Latin by Dugdale, and are reproduced later in this chapter, with their English translation:

Carta Emmae Hai
[*Ex ipso autog, penes Ric. Robinson de Thikhed ar. anno 1652.*]

> *OMNIBUS sanctae matris ecclesiae filiis ego Emma Hai salutem. Sciatis me et haeredes meos concessisse et hac praesenti carta confirmasse Deo et sanctae Mariae de Thiched et sanctimonialibus ibidem Deo servientibus unambovatam terrae in Cotingwit quam Pigot et haeredes sui praedictis sanctimonialibus dederunt, et unum toftum in Crossum, ita liberê et quietè de me et haeredibus meis, sicut praedictus Pigot et haeredes sui praedictis sanctimonialibus carta sua confirmaverunt. His testibus, Rad. Salvage, Willielmo de Murrers, Hamone de Skipwic, Hugone de Boulton, Willi elmo filio Petri, Willielmo Hai, Willielmo de Belebia, et multis aliis.*

To all the daughters of the church of Saint Mary, I, Emma Hay, greetings. Know that me and my heirs by this present charter have granted to God and Saint Mary of Thickhead and the nuns there serving one oxgang of land that Pigot and his heirs gave to the said nuns, and one toft in Crossom, free and exempt from me and my heirs, as the aforesaid Pigot and his heirs confirmed to the said nuns by his charter.

Carta Hugonis de Booltun
[*ibid.*]

> SCIANT omnes, tam praesentes quam futuri, quod ego Hugo de Boolton et Cecilia uxor mea, concessu haeredum nostrorum, dedimus et concessimus, et hac praesenti carta nostra confirmavimus, Deo et sanctae Mariae de Thicheved, et monialibus Ibidem Deo servientibus, in puram et per petuam elemosinam, cum Isonda filia nostra totam partem nostram in castellaria et balliva de Queldric, cum omnibus pertinentiis, et duas acras terrae extra ballivam, unde capita extendunt se versus mariscum; et unam acram terrae; simi liter toftum unum juxta toftum Willielmi Muns; et que relam quam habui apud praedictam domum de terra, scilicet infra clausturam ejusdem domus, scilicet de wasto domini regis Ricardi, quietam clamavimus. Has praenominatas terras praedictae moniales liberê et quietè, pacifice et ho norifice, possidebunt, cum communi pastura, et omnibus aisiamentis, cum libero introitu et exitu et omnibus liber tatibus ejusdem villae pertinentibus. Hiis testibus, Odone capellano, Johanne de Birkin, Willielmo Aguillun, Willielmo de Murrers, Galfrido de Fiteling, Ricardo de Averenches, Hamundo de Duffeld, Gerardo clerico, Petro de Auvers, et multis aliis.

Let all persons, both now and in future, know that I Hugh Bolton Hugh and Cecily my wife, and our heirs, have given and granted and by this present charter confirmed, to God and St. Mary of Thicheved and the nuns there serving God, in pure and perpetual alms, with our daughter, Isonda, the whole of our part of the bailiwick of the castle in Queldric, with all its appurtenances, and outside of the bailiwick the two acres of land, extending towards the marsh; and an acre of land; similarly a toft next to the toft of William Muns; and the suit which he had at the said house and ground, namely within the boundaries of the toft, namely the waste of King Richard, quietly. The above-mentioned lands, the nuns aforesaid to take possession of, freely, quietly, peaceably, and honorably, with common pasture, with all easements and free entry and exit of the same town, and pertaining to all the holy sisters. These witnesses: Odone the chaplain; John of Birkin; William Aguillun; William of Murrers; Geoffrey of Fiteling; Richard de Averenches; Hamo of Duffield; Gerard the clerk; Peter of Auvers, and many others.

Taking the above gifts in order:

Roger son of Roger

The first name in the charter of confirmation is without question the name of the founder, whose foundation grant was made before he died in 1180. The land in 'Tikeheved' was almost certainly wild and uncultivated. If cultivated it was usual to give it as so many oxgangs (or bovates), i.e. land that could be ploughed. The name 'Tikeheved' suggests it was land covered in thicket, usually of alder, hazel or willow, which is still quite common in the marshy areas of the Ouse and Derwent area today, and situated on a head, or loop in the River Derwent. The amount of land was not given at this stage but later deeds, after it had been cleared of the thicket, confirmed that it amounted to ten oxgangs. Of course, the nuns would have little income from such land; at best small amounts from the sale of withies (flexible willow stems used in thatching and basketry) as the land was being cleared. They therefore needed some land that they could farm or lease quickly so they could have an immediate income, and this was provided by the second part of the grant, that of four oxgangs of land in West Cottingwith. But four oxgangs would not be enough to support even the smallest of convents, so it is almost certain that the second grant in the charter of confirmation was made at the same time. The charter of confirmation also refers to a separate grant by Roger son of Roger of one oxgang in Goodmanham.

Thicket Priory was dedicated to the Virgin Mary, as was common in nunneries, and in all probability the dedication was decided at its foundation, but confirmation is lacking. Roger son of Roger died before 1180.

Thomas son of Roger

Brother to Roger son of Roger, gave half a carucate of land (equal to four oxgangs) in West Cottingwith, By 1190 Thomas son of Roger had died, as in that year Thomas, son of Thomas son of Roger, paid 100s. for entry into his father's lands in Aughton and Goodmanham of which Roger [presumably Roger de Hay] was disseising him. Thomas son of Thomas did not live long after, and had died by 1196.

Picot (Pigot)

Picot held land in West Cottingwith, and in the charter of confirmation he granted one oxgang of land there. In the later charter of Emma Hay she confirmed Picot's gift (spelt Pigot in the charter of Emma) and added that his original charter also included one toft in Crossom. This confirmation by Emma Hay shows that Picot held the land of Emma, and was her tenant. As Emma was the heir of Roger son of Roger it is almost certain that Picot held the land under Roger son of Roger in the earlier charter of confirmation. This Picot was almost certainly Picot de Lascelles of Escrick, a parish adjacent to Wheldrake and Thorganby, and if confirmed would place the foundation of Thicket Priory during the reign of Henry II, as Picot de Lascelles was dead by Michaelmas 1179. Picot's son and heir, Roger de Lascelles, would grant further land to Thicket Priory, as we shall see later.

Geoffrey de Fitling (Fitelingham, Ficelingham) and Hugh de Bolton

Geoffrey de Fitling and Hugh de Bolton married the two daughters and heiresses of Thomas Darel of Wheldrake, Beatrice and Cecilly, respectively. Thomas Darel held Wheldrake under the Percys in 1166 and his holding passed to his daughters. Geoffrey de Fitling's son, also a Geoffrey, took the name Darel, and was the ancestor of the subsequent Darels of Wheldrake. In the charter of confirmation Geoffrey and Hugh granted an essart (a form of assart, land recovered from forest for cultivation) out of the king's waste . They also both granted two oxgangs each in Wheldrake.

In addition, by a separate charter, Hugh, along with his wife Cecily and their daughter Isonda granted the whole of their part of the bailiwick of the castle in Queldric [Wheldrake], and two acres of land outside of the bailiwick and an acre of land, and a toft next to the toft of William Muns, and the suit which he had at the said house and ground, i.e. within the boundaries of the toft, namely the waste [land] of King Richard. This mention of the waste [land] of King Richard dates the suit to his reign, 1189x1199, but the charter of Hugh, Cecily and Isonda must be later, probably c. 1200–1201.

Emma, sister of Roger son of Roger

In the confirmation charter, Emma, sister to Roger son of Roger, had given an oxgang of land to the priory in Goodmanham. At the time of the confirmation charter all of the descendants of Roger son of Alured had died: Roger son of Roger; Thomas son of Roger; and his son Thomas; and Emma. As both of her brothers and her nephew Thomas, son of Thomas son of Roger had predeceased Emma she was left as the sole heir to her father's lands, which in turn descended to the de Hay family by her marriage to Roger de Hay.

Following her marriage, now as Emma Hay, she confirmed the grant to Thicket Priory made by Picot in West Cottingwith, and also a toft in Crossom, which was not mentioned in the confirmation charter. These confirmations indicate that Picot was her under-tenant in West Cottingwith.

The inheritance of Roger son of Roger did not pass directly to Emma on his death which occurred before 1190, instead passing briefly to his brother Thomas, who was deceased in 1190, then to Thomas son of Thomas, who was dead without issue before 1196. This left Emma as the sole heir of her father, Roger son of Alured.

Emma's husband, Roger de Hay, appears to have held the inheritance of Thomas son of Thomas until he came of age, as in 1191 Thomas paid into the exchequer for entry into his father's lands, of which he was disseised by Roger [de Hay]. Roger de Hay was dead in 1196, and his widow Emma died around 1200. The family's lands in Yorkshire then passed to their son, Thomas de Hay.

Emma of Dilolton (Diholton)

This lady is something of a mystery. Apart from her appearing in the charter of confirmation as having granted to Thicket one oxgang of land in Wheldrake, she is not mentioned again in contemporary, earlier or later records. The placename 'Dilolton' is also a mystery. However, in the *Inspeximus* and confirmation of the charter of King John to Thicket Priory granted by King Edward I in May 1285, the name is rendered 'Diholton', but with the same problems of identification as 'Dilolton'.

Richard Malbis (Mallebisse)

As mentioned previously, Geoffrey de Fitling and Hugh de Bolton married the two daughters and heiresses of Thomas Darel of Wheldrake. Thomas Darel held Wheldrake under the Percys in 1166, but under the division of William de Percy's estates in 1175 Maud de Percy, Countess of Warwick, gave her nephew, Richard Malbis, the service of Thomas Darel's heirs, his daughters Beatrice and Cecily, and the Malbis family became the lords of Wheldrake, with the Darels as their vassals.

At some point Richard Malbis granted the precinct of the castle (*castellano*) of Wheldrake to Thicket Priory, as John Burton informs us that Sibilla, prioress of Thickeved, and the convent thereof, quitclaimed around 1211-1214 all their right to the precinct of the castle, with one acre of land, and four other acres, that Richard Malebisse had given them.

In order to date the grant of the precinct of the castle to Thicket Priory by Richard Malbis, and the bailiwick of the castle by Thomas Darel's heirs, we must look to the Chronicle of Roger of Howden, which tells us that Richard Malbis was granted a licence dated 31 March 1200, to fortify a castle he was building in Queldric (Wheldrake), but the licence was revoked due to pressure from the garrison and sheriff of York, and the building was never completed. It was this setback that probably persuaded Malbis and his vassals to divest themselves of the uncompleted castle, and donate it to Thicket Priory, probably during the latter part of 1200 or during 1201.

Walter de Percy

In February 1218/19 Walter granted to Thicket a carucate of land in Sand Hutton, and in addition three oxgangs lying in Norton fields between the land of Maud of Flammavill and land held of Walter by Thomas le Large; a toft held by Wymark; and two parts of a toft held by Godard: to hold to the prioress and her successors and her church of S. Mary of Thickeheved for ever, in frankalmoign, quit of all secular service. In 1219 Walter was recorded in the Fine Rolls and Pipe Rolls as owing the king one mark for a carucate of land in Sand Hutton, held of the prioress of Thicket.

William, son of Peter

According to John Burton, in 12 Henry III (28 October 1227-27 October 1228), William son of Peter, granted to the prioress and convent of Thicket ten oxgangs of land in Cottingwith, but it is not recorded in the *Feet of Fines for Yorkshire*. However, there is a fine, 15 Henry III (28 October 1230-27 October 1231), between Eve, the prioress of Thicket, and Agnes the daughter of Peter (and sister to William son of Peter) concerning ten oxgangs of land in Cottingwith which the prioress and her church of Tykeheved hold by the gift of William son of Peter, in frankalmoign. The prioress to receive Agnes into all benefactions and prayers henceforth.

This fine was the result of an earlier case in an Assize at York, dated 8 June 1231, in which the prioress of Tykeved summoned Agnes daughter of Peter to warrant ten oxgangs of land in Cottingwith, for which the prioress held the charter of William son of Peter, his heir; and for default of warranty the prioress was compelled to do suit at the Wapentake and County Courts. The prioress claimed one hundred shillings damages, and produced the charter by which William son of Peter gave to the nuns of Tykeheved in frankalmoign, and warranted that he and his heirs would acquit the nuns of all secular services. Agnes came and admitted the charter and warranty, and said that she would acquit the prioress of all services, as the charter witnessed. They reached a concord and had a cyrograph, and the prioress remitted her damages.

This fine presents a problem, as in *Kirkby's Inquest* for the year 1284-5 the total holding of the prioress in Cottingwith was ten oxgangs when previously we have seen that Roger son of Roger gave four oxgangs there, as did his brother, Thomas son of Roger, and a further one oxgang by Picot, totalling nine oxgangs. It was theorised that this was not a new grant of William son of Peter, but a confirmation of the nine oxgangs gifted by Roger, Thomas and Picot at the foundation, and that the missing one oxgang was the land in Thicket that Roger son of Roger had given also at the foundation. This theory is more than reasonable, as the heir of these grants, Emma Hay, passed to her descendants any outstanding obligations relating to this land, and in September 1280 her great grandson, German Hay, agreed with Joan, prioress of Thicket, that he would do the king's service arising from the messuage and 10 oxgangs she held of him in Thicket and Cottingwith.

Later Grants from 1250 to the Dissolution

Godfrey de Melsa (Meaux) and Isabel de Acun

This grant is derived. Thicket Priory is listed as holding Lepton (Leppington, in the parish of Scayingham) at the Dissolution. We know that Thicket held land in Lepington after the death of Godfrey de Melsa, but before his widow, Isabel de Acun, had died. This constrains the dates to circa 1249x1294. No grant has been found to indicate who granted Thicket Priory this land in Leppington, but in the absence of any evidence it is assumed it was the lords of Leppington, Godfrey de Melsa, or his wife Isabel de Acun, who was known to German Hay.

Ellerton Priory

In 1264, with the consent of German de Hay, the patron of Thickeved, an agreement was made between the prior and convent of Ellerton, and the prioress and nuns of Thicket, namely: that the prior and convent would confirm to the nuns certain lands held of German's fee in West Cottingwith and Crossum, for which the prioress and nuns would give a toft in West Cottingwith, and two selions of land in Lundcroft

Thicket needed the confirmation of Ellerton Priory for the lands they held in West Cottingwith and Crossom, as in the *Nomina Villarum* of 1316 it is recorded that Ellerton Priory was the lord of those places.

Rather than being a grant of land, this confirmation actually cost Thicket two pieces of property. The toft they gave was almost certainly the one given by Picot in Crossom, but how the two selions in Lundcroft came into Thicket's possession is unclear.

Fountains Abbey

It has been mentioned previously that around 1211–1214, Sybil, the prioress of Thicket, quitclaimed all the right of Thicket Priory to the precinct of the castle, with one acre of land, and four other acres, that Richard Malbis had given them. But in 1290, Robert the abbot of Fountains and the convent thereof, gave to Joan, prioress of Thicheved, and the convent thereof, and their successors, five acres of land next to Thickevedrave, near the land of the said prioress. It is unclear if this was the same five acres that Sybil had quitclaimed. In the *Memorandum Book of Fountains*, it was noted that in the period 1446–1458 Thicket paid seven pence for one acre of land in Thikheued Rayn per annum, and the same for one acre of land in Moscrofte.

Roger de Lascelles

By an escheat in the 18th of Edw I, [20 November 1289-19 November 1290], it appears that Roger de Lascelles held land in Escrick at that time of the prioress of Thicket. An *inquisition ad quod damnum* was held to determine if an alienation of this land would damage the king, which returned in the negative, and consequently Roger was granted a licence, 8 April 1291, to alienate in mortmain five score acres of land in Escrick to the prioress and nuns of Thickeheved.

Although not mentioned in the inquisition or licence, Joan, the prioress of Thicket, was also granted a free tenement in Escrick by Roger, and in 1300 she raised a case in the Court of Common Pleas against the heirs of Roger to exonerate her of the service which the Abbat of St. Mary's, York required for the free tenement she held of them in Escrick.

William le Gra

William le Gra of York sold by Fine a messuage and 1000 acres of marsh at Sand Hutton (*pro mess. Et M. acris marisci in Sand-Hoton juxta Stainford Bridge*) to Joan, Prioress of Thikheued. William remitted and quitclaimed in court for himself and his heirs to the Prioress, her successors and her church and will warrant. For £20 sterling. By the king's command. Dated: 32 Edw I, [20 November 1303-19 November 1304].

Thomas de Alwathorpe (Alwarthorp, Alverthorp)

On the 5 November 1318, at York, the prioress and nuns of Thykeheved were granted a licence to acquire, in mortmain (the perpetual, inalienable ownership of real estate by a corporation, in this case, Thicket Priory), lands, tenements and rents to the value of 10 marks a year. The prioress at this time was Alice de

Alverthorpe, and the application for a licence was normally the first step in a pre-agreed grant by a benefactor. In 12 Edw. I (08 Jul 1318 – 07 Jul 1319) Thomas de Alwathorpe, applied for a licence to alienate (to sell to another person or corporation) in mortmain a house, land and rent in York, West Cottingwith and Green Hammerton. Accordingly an *inquisition ad quod damnum* was conducted to determine if this would be prejudicial to the crown, or anyone else, and being in the negative a licence was duly granted, which read:

> Licence for the alienation in mortmain to the prioress and nuns of Thikeheved (or Tykeheved) by Thomas de Alwarthorpe of York of a messuage, an oxgang of land, and 15s. 1d. of rent in York, West Cottyngwith and Grenhamerton, which are held of the prioress and are worth in all their issues according to their true value 20s. as appears by an inquisition made by the sheriff of York, in part satisfaction of a licence granted to them to acquire in mortmain lands, tenements and rents to the value of 10 marks a year.

This was not the first gift to a religious house that Thomas de Alwathorpe had made. In 1311 he had granted 5 marks of rent in York to a chaplain to celebrate divine service in the Church of All Saints, Ousegate, York, for the souls of Roger Haget and Ellen his wife, and of the grantor and Isabella his sister, and of their ancestors.

But who was Thomas de Alwathorpe? In 1307 he was appointed to the custody of the smaller piece of the seal for the recognisances of debts for the City of York. In 1311 he was M.P. for York, and from 1315 he was the clerk of John Malbis, late Sheriff of York, and engaged on the king's service collecting fees and dues to the crown from the county, and was bailiff of the City of York in 1316 and 1317.

Thomas's sister, Isabella, has already been mentioned, but it remains to be seen what relation Thomas was to the prioress of Thicket, Alice de Alverthorp, but they were most likely close kin, if not another sister of Thomas. Alice de Alverthorpe resigned (probably due to old age) in 1335, after serving as prioress from 1309.

Robert de Lyndesey

Robert de Lyndesey of York confirmed a donation of 10s. annual rent from a tenement in Colbergate, York, to the nuns of Thikheved which [mutilated] … de Feryby and Juliana his wife and mother of the said Robert had granted to them for fourteen years. Dated at York, the Saturday after the feast of St. Nicholas, 8 Edw III (10 December 1334).

Robert de Youlton or de Yolton

At the inquisition of Robert de Yolton held in York 23 September 1350, it was found that he had the service of a bovate of land in Yolton, held time out of mind by the prioress of Thikheved in frankalmoign.

Sir Robert Aske

In 1522 Sir Robert de Aske, knight, granted a yearly rent of 7s. 4d. for an annual obit 'for the souls of Robert de Aske, one of the late patrons of this house, and Elizabeth his wife'.

Foundation and Early Grants

Place	Donor(s)	Grant	Year
Thickhead	Roger Fitz Roger	Territory of. Later defined (post-clearing) as 10 oxgangs	Before 1204
W. Cottingwith	Roger Fitz Roger	4 oxgangs	Before 1204
Goodmanham	Roger Fitz Roger	1 oxgang	Before 1204
W. Cottingwith	Thomas Fitz Roger	½ carucate	Before 1204
W. Cottingwith	Picot	1 oxgang	Before 1204
W. Cottingwith	Geoffrey de Ficelingham and Hugh de Bolton	Essart of land of the king's waste	Before 1204
W. Cottingwith	William, son of Peter	10 oxgangs	Before 1231
Goodmanham	Emma, sister of Roger Fitz Roger	1 oxgang	Before 1204

Place	Donor(s)	Grant	Year
Wheldrake	Geoffrey de Ficelingham and Hugh de Bolton	2 oxgangs each	Before 1204
Wheldrake	Emma de Ditholton	1 oxgang	Before 1204
Crossum	Picot	1 oxgang	Before 1200
Wheldrake	Hugh de Bolton with his daughter, Isolda	His part of the castle of Wheldrake, with 2 acres and a toft	1189x1199
Wheldrake	Richard Mallebisse	The castle of Wheldrake, with 5 acres	Before 1214
Sand Hutton	Walter de Percy	1 carucate	Before 1219
Norton	William de Percy	3 oxgangs	Before 1219

Note: All of the above endowments were probably granted around the same time, during or shortly after the foundation, which was as early as Richard I (1189x1199) but more likely earlier, temp. Henry II, if Picot is identical with Picot de Lascelles (d. 1179), the father of Roger de Lascelles.

I suspect Thicket was founded by Roger son of Roger, in the period following the death of his father, Roger son of Alured, who had died by 1162, placing the probable foundation date as 1162x1179.

Later Grants

Place	Donor(s)	Grant	Year
West Cottingwith and Crossum	Prior and Convent of Ellerton	Confirmation of the lands held by Thicket Priory. Thicket yields one toft in West Cottingwith, and two selions of land in Lundcroft	1264
York	Unknown	Rent-charge of 4s. 6d. per annum upon lands in York	c. 1279
Thikehed	Abbot and Convent of Fountains	5 acres of land at Thicket	1290
Escrick	Roger de Lascelles	5 score acres of land in Escrick	c. 1291
York and Sand Hutton	William la Gra of York	Lands in York, and a very large tract of land in the marsh at Sand Hutton	1304
Benetland	Unknown	Thicket Priory held this Lordship in *Kirkby's Inquest*	c. 1315/16
York, West Cottingwith and Greenhamerton	Thomas de Alwathorpe of York	A messuage, a bovate of land, and 15s. 1d. of rent in York, West Cottyngwith and Grenhamerton	c. 1318/19
York	Robert de Lyndesey of York	10s. annual rent from a tenement in Colbergate, York	1334
Yolton	Robert de Yolton	One oxgang	Before 1350
Obit	Sir Robert de Aske	A yearly rent of 7s. 4d. for an annual obit for Robert de Aske, one of the late patrons of this house, and Eliz. his wife	1522

Other Property Interests

Apart from property that was granted to the priory, Thicket had at least one other property interest. After 1454 Thicket Priory leased Talkan Tower in York, one of the city's posterns on the River Foss which was later replaced with the Fishergate Postern Tower. It is not known to what purpose this lease was applied. It may have been rooms for the prioress when she was in York on business, or an office for the priory's receiver in York.

Testamentary Bequests

The numbers of bequests to Thicket are few in number, given the small size of the priory, and the sparsely populated location.

1398: Sir Thomas Ughtred bequeathed in his will to the nuns of Thicket, 40s. to pray for the souls of himself, his wife Katherine and William his son.

1402: Sir John Depeden bequeathed in his will to the holy nuns of Thicket, 20s. to pray for the souls of himself and his wife Elizabeth.

1404: Walter Berghe bequeathed in his will to the priory and convent of Thicket, 20s.

1494/5: Sir Brian Roucliffe of Cowthorpe, one of the Barons of the Exchequer, bequeathed in his will to the priory and convent of Thicket, half a mark.

1500: Edmund Thwaites of Lund, Esq., bequeathed in his will to the prioress of Thicket, 20s.

1530: Edward Saltmarshe of West Cottingwith, bequeathed in his will to the prioress of Thicket and her sisters, 3s.

Testamentary Burials

It is clear that Thicket Priory had a burial ground, or burial facilities within their chapel. The evidence for this comes in the last wills and testaments of Yorkshire testators wishing to be buried at the priory. Unfortunately, none give the precise location (e.g. in the burial ground, or in the quire of the chapel).

The following testamentary burials are from the indices to Wills in the York Registry, 1389–1553.

1405: Henry Undirwynd, to be buried in Thykhed Abbey (*sic*), vol. 3, fol. 242.

1438: William Gibson of Queldryk [Wheldrake], to be buried in Thikhede Monastery (*sic*), vol. 3, fol. 540.

1438: John Langton, chaplain, to be buried in the Convent of Thikhede, vol. 3, fol. 593.

1491: John Beltonson of Cottingwith, chaplain, to be buried in Thikehede Priory, vol. 5, fol. 405.

The Construction of the Priory

The size and construction methods of the original buildings that comprised Thicket Priory at its foundation in the late twelfth century is not known with certainty, but it is likely that the priory consisted of a modest wooden main building, with thatched roof, capable of accommodating the minimum number of nuns for a priory, i.e. twelve, and some outbuildings dedicated to livestock and agriculture.

The priory was also granted murage (a toll for the repair or constructions of walls) 13 Edward I, but it is not clear if this was for a containing wall around the priory or for flood defences. Over the next 300 years we know the building was improved and expanded, with the addition of an upper floor, the replacement of thatched roofs with tiles and lead, the introduction of glass windows to replace shuttered windows, and the construction of further outbuildings. It is clear that the internal partition walls maintained their original construction given the ready nearby supply of withies, mud and straw.

A Typical Late Medieval Benedictine Cloister

Fortunately, we have a very detailed description of Thicket Priory taken from the Surveys conducted by the Visitors sent out by Henry VIII prior to the Dissolution of the Monasteries, which clearly shows these improvements, and gives the description of every room on both floors of the priory, plus the outbuildings, with some rooms having construction details.

Thicket Priory was described thus by the Visitors:

> *The church, 60 feet long by internally 18 foot broad, with a low roof covered with lead, with 5 glass windows containing 44 feet of glass, with 16 stalls in the quire, and the high altar, 2 in the quire and 1 underneath.*

> *Item: The cloister, at the north end of the church, 60 feet square by 6 feet broad, covered with tiles over 1 part and 3 parts under chambers.*

> *Item: The chapter house, at the east side of the cloister, 12 feet long by 8 feet broad, with a little glass window, 4 feet of glass.*

> *Item: Two other low chambers by the same.*

> *Item: The dorter [dormitory] over the cloister and chapter and chambers, 60 feet long by 15 feet broad, covered with tiles.*

> *Item: The brewing house and bulting house [the large room where meal was sifted], all the length of the north side of the cloister, and 10 feet broad.*

> *Item: An old bakehouse by the same, 20 feet square, daubed walls all covered with thak [daub and wattle].*

> *Item: The garner [where corn was stored] over the brewhouse and the cloister, 51 feet long by 18 feet broad, with timber walls covered with tiles.*

> *Item: A new wood house at the west side of the cloister, 32 feet long by 6 feet broad, and timber walls.*

Item: A chamber over the same, 32 feet long by 12 feet broad, timber walls, covered with tiles, and the floor but half boarded for it is not yet finished.

Item: The new parler [a place where the rule of silence was relaxed and where business could be conducted; a place where merchants could buy and sell to the priory] at the west side by the church door, 24 feet long by 20 feet broad, with one bay window glassed containing 30 feet of glass and 3 other little glass windows, and timber walls with a chimney.

Item: A little buttery by the same.

Item: A new chamber over the parler, 24 feet long by 20 feet broad, with a chimney, timber walls covered with tiles and a glass window containing 12 feet of glass.

Item: A little chamber by the same over the buttery and cloister.

Item: A little cheesehouse between the parler and the kitchen.

Item: The new kitchen 18 feet long by 12 feet broad with a fair chimney, timber walls, covered with tiles.

Item: A chamber over the kitchen called the kitchen chamber or cheese chamber, 18 feet long by 12 feet broad, plastered floor, good timber walls, covered with tiles and no glass.

Item: A little chamber by the same, 10 feet square covered with tiles.

Item: A chamber at the nether end of the church, 14 feet square, with a chimney, a little glass window, timbered walls, covered with tiles.
A little chamber by the same, 10 feet square covered with tiles.

Item: The milk house, 8 feet square, by the kitchen.

Item: A little larder, 10 feet long and 6 feet broad.

Item: The low hall, 20 feet long by 14 feet broad with a fair chimney, a glass window somewhat broken, timber walls, covered with tiles.

Item: A little buttery at the upper end of the same by the parler, 12 feet long by 8 feet broad.

Item: The parler at the upper end of the hall, 16 feet square, with a chimney, a bay window glassed, 10 feet of glass, and timber walls and sealed above with wainscot.

Item: A chamber over the parler, 20 feet long by 17 feet broad, with a chimney, a glass window, timber walls, covered with tiles.

Item: Another buttery, 12 feet long by 10 feet broad, with a little chamber or house by the same.

Item: Another chamber over the buttery, 16 feet square, with a little glass window of 6 feet of glass, timber walls, covered with tiles.

Item: A dovecot before the hall door, 12 feet square, timber walls, decayed, ill covered with slates.

Item: A guest stable, 22 feet long by 12 feet broad, timber walls, covered with tiles.

Item: An old hay barn, 60 foot long by 20 feet broad, ill daubed walls, decayed, and ill covered with thak.

Item: A corn barn, 24/4 feet long by 20 feet broad, timber walls covered with thak.

Item: An old stable for workhorses, 20 feet long, and 14 feet broad, old daubed walls, covered with thak.

Item: An ox-house and cow-house together 24/16 feet long by 16 feet broad, daubed walls, covered with flak.

Item: The priest's chamber, 12 feet square, daubed walls covered with thak.

Item: The kiln house, 24 feet long by 14 feet broad, daubed walls, covered with thak.

Item: An old swinecot.

The references to *the new bakehouse, the new wood house, the new parler* and *the new chamber*, while still retaining the old rooms of the same names, all clearly show expansion.

It is known that the priory had a mill, and it is mentioned in the Survey. It was not within the priory precincts, but was probably close by. In 1683 and 1703 there were fields in West Cottingwith named Mill Hill, and Mill Hill Lands, and in 1757 a Mill Field is mentioned, which all may give clues to the site of the mill. Unfortunately the tithes of Thorganby and West Cottingwith were extinguished by an Enclosure Act in 1810, so the invaluable tithe maps of the 1830s, with their listing of all the fieldnames, were not created.

The floor plans of Thicket Priory that follow, derived from the descriptions in the Visitors' Survey, are scaled and are largely accurate, but doorways, staircases and corridors are not mentioned in the Survey, neither are the placement of the outbuildings, so their placement has been estimated from contemporary surviving priories in England and Europe.

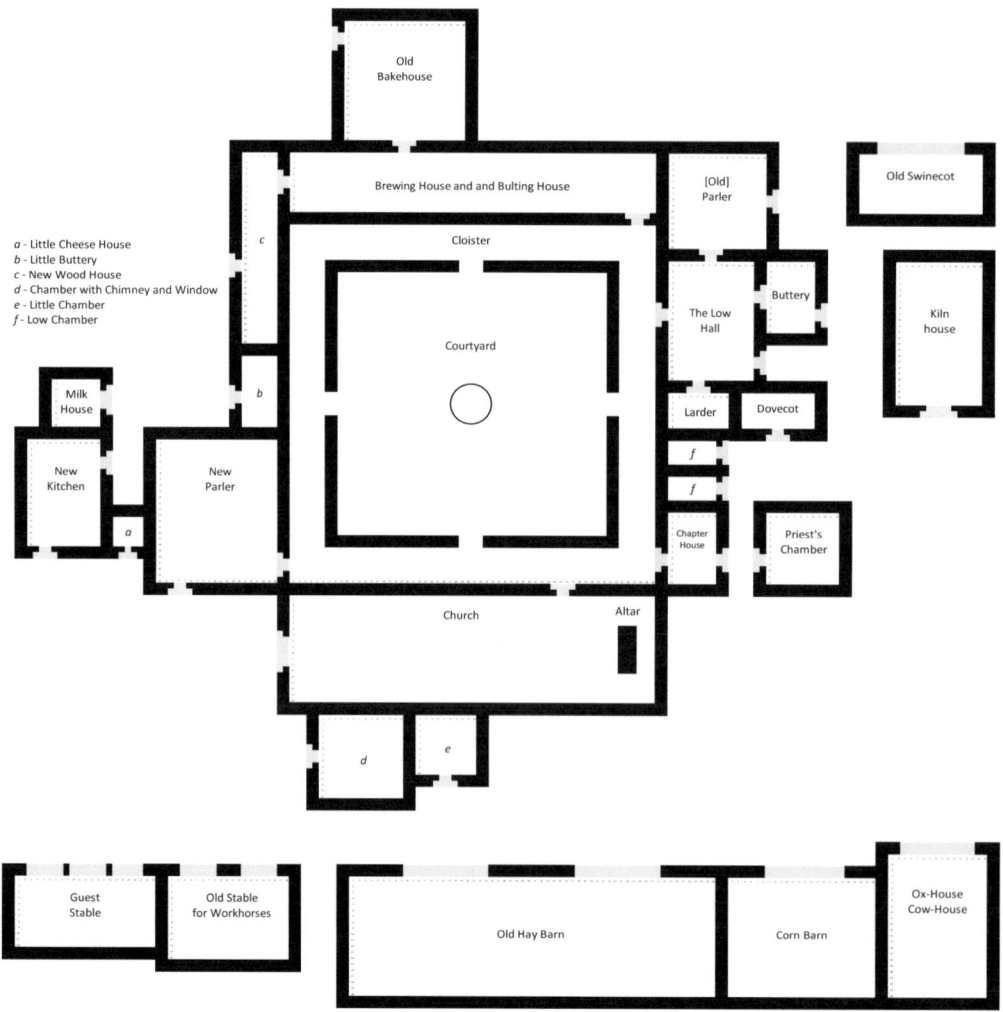

Ground Floor Plan of Thicket Priory

The walls of the upper floor plan are shown in black, while ground floor rooms that are single storey are shown in dark grey, to indicate how the ground floor and upper floor are aligned.

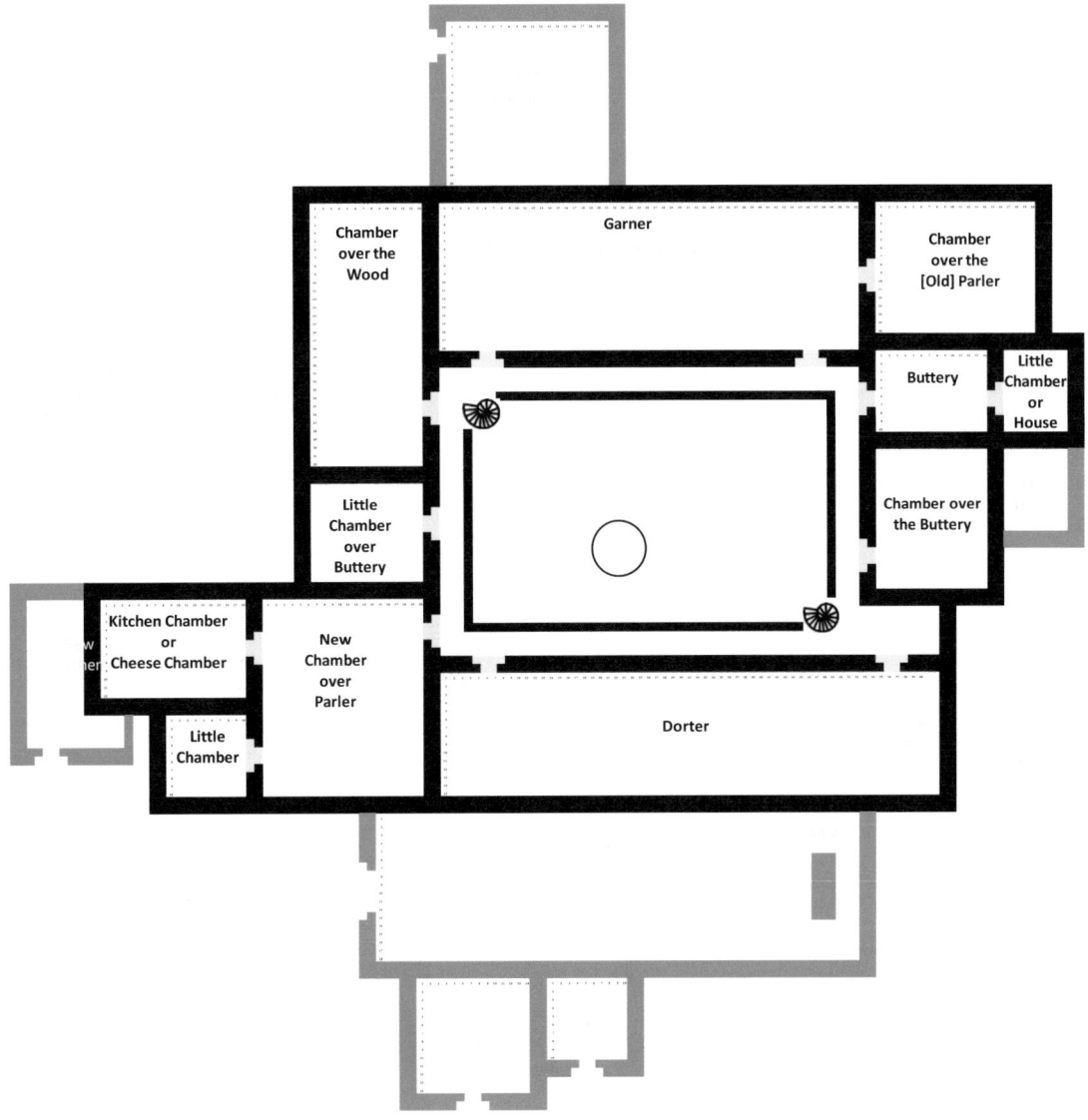

Upper Floor Plan of Thicket Priory

The walls of the upper floor plan are shown in black, while ground floor rooms that are single storey are shown in dark grey, to indicate how the ground floor and upper floor are aligned.

Looking at the layout of the upper floor, one could imagine that the New Chamber over the Parler, and the two chambers off it, likely formed the rooms of the prioress, which was usually a lady of high birth. The nuns would have lived a dormitory life in the Dorter, and guests and the holders of corrodies would occupy the remaining chambers.

The Economy of the Priory

Some of the land granted to Thicket Priory during its foundation and later was heavily wooded, but with mostly low quality trees. This land would have to be assarted (deforested) to turn it into arable agricultural land that could be ploughed or turned to pasture. Some of the donors to Thicket mentioned that they had royal licences to deforest land they had donated, but still much needed to be done, and the nuns set about having their lands deforested, some by labourers for their demesne land, and some by potential tenants who would clear the land then lease it from the priory.

Much of the land between the Ouse and Derwent needed deforesting to make it productive, often without a direct licence by the king, but in 1234 King Henry III imposed a blanket fine on the whole of the Ouse and Derwent area for deforestation, but in quiet and full satisfaction. The fine was set at eight hundred marks, and the portion allocated to Thicket was a modest six marks and four shillings. Later, on a petition from the queen, Thicket was pardoned three marks of the total sum.

In the section, *The Construction of the Priory*, the names of the various rooms give us an insight of the sort of work the nuns were engaged in, and it is immediately apparent that the nuns were involved in modest agriculture. They did not farm all their land themselves of course, just enough for their own needs, and the rest was farmed by tenants.

Of particular importance was grain, which they stored in the Corn Barn, before threshing, with the resulting grain being stored in the Garner. After the grain was ground in their windmill the flour would be sifted in the Bulting House, and then used in the Bakehouse for their bread, and in the Kiln for drying before malting, then on to the Brewing House for the brewing of light ale for their own consumption and that of their servants, and possibly for local sale.

They also had a modest amount of livestock. The oxen would have been used for ploughing, and their cows used for milk which was stored in the Milk House, before skimming and churning to make cheese which they stored in the Cheesehouse. During the winter the oxen would be kept in the Ox and Cow Houses. The nuns also kept pigs, penned in their Swinecot; and pigeons in their Dovecot, used for their eggs and meat, and their guano for fertiliser and tanning hides; and sheep, mainly for their wool, which they would use locally, with the excess being exported.

Thicket's cattle would have been grazed on pasture, mostly consisting of meadows alongside the river, which was termed locally as Ings. In the early summer the grass would be cut for hay, which was stored for the winter period in the Hay Barn. Of course, having a navigable river on your doorstep has its advantages in terms of fish, fisheries and transport, but there were disadvantages. The low-lying area of Wheldrake and Thorganby parishes that bordered the river were prone to seasonal flooding, which if managed carefully could be turned into an advantage, as the river brought nutrients with it to enrich these lands when flooding occurred. But occasionally, the flooding was so severe that great damage was done, as was the case in July 1343, when the prioress of Thicket complained that the priory and their tenants have suffered damage from floods, due to lack of repair of the banks of a sewer. An Inquisition into the complaint concluded that the bishop of Durham and the prebendary of Rikhale [Riccall] should heighten the banks at the mouth of the sewer. Again, in October, 1484, Archbishop Rotherham issued a letter asking for help for the house of the nuns of Thicket, whose fields and pasturage had been inundated by floods, and who had suffered much loss by the death of their cattle.

At first sight the reader may be forgiven for thinking that the nuns also made butter, which they may have done, but the rooms called the 'Little Buttery' were in fact larders, i.e. rooms for storing food and drink. The nuns' buttery and the butteries for guests were kept separately.

Thicket, along with several other Yorkshire nunneries, exported a modest amount of wool to Flanders and Italy, with Arden exporting ten sacks, Swine eight sacks, and Thicket four sacks. With the Derwent being a commonly used route for the wool trade between the North and East Ridings and the great port of Hull, it would have been easy for the nuns to have their sacks of wool laden at one of the staithes in Cottingwith, though weirs on the river sometimes caused difficulties. Alternatively the wool could be carried to York less than ten miles away, by the wool collectors of the larger religious houses who operated in the area, or directly by the agents of the Italian wool merchants.

It is not known what route was actually taken, or if the wool of Thicket was collected from the priory itself, but the prioress of Arden, a Benedictine nunnery thirty miles north of Thicket, said this about wool from her house: 'the Italians used to send their attorneys to Arden, within the said priory, who put the said wool in sarplers and packed it and caused it to be packed at the expense of the same merchants...and to be carried to the wool-house of Byland at Thorpe, for delivery to the said merchants.' But usually delivery was made to Clifton, a suburb of York, where the wool was loaded onto boats and sent down the Ouse to Hull.

With the area around Thicket being within the demesne of Fountains Abbey, and their heavy involvement in the wool trade, it is quite possible that their agents bought the wool from Thicket.

By the fifth or sixth century, Christianity had a scale of taboos on eating terrestrial 'flesh', but western Christians in particular allowed most people to substitute fish on the roughly 130 days (35%) of the year when ideology forbade them meat. This encouraged those who could afford fish to eat it weekly and seasonally.

The main rivers of the East Riding of Yorkshire, the rivers Ouse, Derwent and Hull, all fed fisheries and meres to store the non-migratory species, such as bream, perch, barbel and pike, but also migrants on their seasonal runs, eel especially, and some of these fisheries were mentioned in Domesday, with eel being used as a standard measure of a fishery's value.

Net-caught fish were placed in artificial ponds, called stews, for later consumption, and larger meres, both natural and man-made, were used to stock and breed fish.

The Derwent had several v-shaped weirs in the vicinity of Thicket, not wide enough to prevent river navigation, though there were complaints that sometimes they did. These weirs funnelled fish into a conical basket at the point of the 'v' to trap eel and other fish. The baskets or traps were made from the abundant alder or willow withies.

The nuns of Thicket had both weirs on the Derwent and access to a part of a great mere, known as Alemare or Eelmere in the loop between the old and new courses of the River Derwent, in Wheldrake parish. Eelmere was perhaps aptly named, given that eel was the most plentiful species available.

At Domesday Wheldrake was held of the king by William de Percy as his tenant-in-chief. When William de Percy's estates were divided between his two daughters in 1175 Wheldrake was assigned to the Earl of Warwick, the husband of William's daughter, Maud de Percy. Between c. 1184 (when the Earl of Warwick died, without issue) and c. 1200 Maud gave her nephew, Richard Malbis, the lordship of Wheldrake, and Thomas Darel's heirs thus became Richard's under-tenants. Richard Malbis died in 1210, and before his death he donated all his lands, possessions and rights in Wheldrake to the monks of Fountains Abbey.

Following their acquisition of the lordship of Wheldrake the monks set about extinguishing the rights of their under-tenants, and common rights, to the fisheries in Alemare, and despite some resistance from the more powerful under-tenants, including the Darrell and Hay families, all resistance was overcome and the monks secured sole rights to Alemare. The various surrenders, quitclaims and court cases concerning Alemare give some interesting location detail. It was located in the Ings of Wheldrake, and was connected to the Derwent, possibly by a drain, and bordered Storthwaite on the opposite bank.

Included in the list of surrenders was the quitclaim by Sibilla, the prioress of Thicket, of the priory's rights in Alemare, pertaining to their original foundation grant of Thikeheued, by Roger son of Roger, in return for the abbey's 'counsel and aid'. However, the nuns of Thicket did retain their weir and fishery on the Derwent, which was mentioned again in 1332, when several powerful lords complained that the weirs around Wheldrake and Cottingwith, belonging to the monks of Fountains and the nuns of Thicket, obstructed river traffic, to their damage. Interestingly, Fountains Abbey complained about the weir of Thicket, and Thicket complained about the weirs of Fountains. There is no further mention of the weir and its fishery, and it is not listed in the Dissolution documents of 1539, nor in the subsequent Letters Patent allocating the site and lands of Ellerton Priory and Thicket Priory to John Aske, in 1542, which did list explicitly the fishery in the Derwent belonging to the dissolved Ellerton Priory.

Thicket Priory occasionally granted corrodies, but always subject to a licence granted by the Archbishop of York. A corrody was similar to the modern practice of paying a lump sum to live the rest of your days in a retirement home, but in one case in Thicket a corrody was granted to a chaplain (a room, food and drink, and a small stipend), in return for his services, for life.

Non-permanent paying residents, or boarders, were also taken in, but again subject to a licence, and these will be discussed in the next section, and some were female children taken in for education, with a view to eventual admittance into the sisterhood. More of a monastic prep-school than a school in the general sense, but some children were sent there purely for education.

Internal Community

The earliest known prioress of Thicket Priory, Sibilla, occurs between 1214 and 1218, and could possibly have been the first prioress, but it is more likely that another preceded her. The widowed mother of the three founders, the children of Roger son of Alured, is never mentioned, but it should be considered possible that they had their widowed mother installed as the first prioress

Sibilla

This prioress, the first recorded prioress of Thicket, occurs for the first time when she quitclaimed to Fountains Abbey the precinct and bailiwick of Wheldrake Castle. A witness to this quitclaim was Henry de Redman, Sheriff of York, who held the post of sheriff 1211-1214.

The next occurrence is dated 16 February, 1218/9, when Walter de Percy, claimant, and Sybil, Prioress of Thickeheved, tenant, were involved in a Feet of Fine concerning a carucate of land in Sandhouton.

A Sibilla Hay occurs in a case of *Novel Disseisin* in October 1227, as demandent (*aramiavit*) against Richard de Murers, concerning a tenement in Elvington, which borders Wheldrake. As the Hay family in the person of Roger de Hay (d. 1190-96) originally came from Sussex, and only appeared in this area of Yorkshire when Roger settled in North Cave following his marriage to Emma (d. c. 1200), the sister of Roger son of Roger, it is very probable that Sibilla Hay was a daughter of Roger de Hay and Emma, and sister to the known son of Roger and Emma, Thomas Hay (d. 1226-7). This Sibilla Hay does not occur again in contemporary records.

Given that the patrons of religious houses often had installed one of their own kin as head, it is possible that Sibilla Hay who occurs in 1227 was the Sibilla, the prioress of Thicket in 1214, but was acting in a private suit, and using her full name. It must be stressed that this is just a theory, and more evidence is needed to confirm it, one way or the other.

Eve

Only one occurrence found, 12 June 1231, when as plaintiff, and Prioress of Tikeheved, she fined with Agnes, daughter of Peter, *impedient*, concerning ten oxgangs of land in Cottingwith.

Alice

Occurs just twice in passing. She is described as the *late* Prioress in 1279, and again in 1282, both during the time that Henry was Prior of Ellerton, i.e. c. 1250s-1260s.

Joan

Joan occurs in 1279, and also from the day after Michaelmas 1280, when as *querent*, she fined with German Hay to quit her of service in the county and wapentake courts, and to grant her the tenement and lands she holds of him in Thorganby and Cottingwith in free alms.

In 1282, Joan, Prioress of Thycheheved had suit against the Prior of Ellerton, to permit her to have common pasture in Cottingwith which belongs to her free tenement there, and of which Henry, late Prior of Ellerton, unjustly disseised Alice, late Prioress of Thycheheved.

In 1290, Robert, abbot and convent of Fountains, gave to Joan, prioress of Thicheved and the convent thereof, and their successors, five acres of land next to Thickevedrave, near the land of the said prioress. This mention of 'near the land of the said prioress' rather than 'near the land of the said priory', suggests that Joan held land in her own right in the area.

In 1300 Joan claimed against Thomas, son of Ivo de Gra, a house, 3 tofts, 3 oxgangs of land and 5½ acres of wood in Sand Hutton by writ of entry. Joan also claimed against William, another son of Ivo de Gra, the same as above.

Also in 1300: Elizabeth, widow of Roger de Lascelles claimed against the Prioress of Thicheved one third of 100 acres of land in Thickeved as her dower; and Joan, the Prioress of Tykeheved against John de Curewenne, Rober le Conestable and Amice his wife, Robert de Tilliol and Maud his wife, and Ralph FitzRalph and Theophania his wife, to exonerate her of the service which the Abbat of St. Mary's York requires for the free tenement in York she holds of the defendants in Escrick.

Joan occurs for the last time in 1306 in a suit against William, son of Ivo de Gra, concerning seven acres of land, eight acres of meadow, and eight and a half acres of wood in Sand Hutton.

Alice de Alverthorpe

Alice is one of the few prioresses in having fairly precise dates in relation to her election, and her resignation, after serving as prioress for nearly thirty years.

In the register of Archbishop Walter Greenfield, 1306–1315, is an entry dated 12 August 1309, confirming her election, and instructing the Archdeacon or his Official to install.

Alice occurs again in July 1317, when she defended an action by Alice de Wighton, concerning tenements in Thykheved.

On the 5 November 1318, at York, the prioress and nuns of Thykeheved were granted a licence to acquire in mortmain lands, tenements and rents to the value of 10 marks a year. The prioress at this time was Alice de Alverthorpe, and in 12 Edw. I (08 Jul 1318–07 Jul 1319) Thomas de Alwathorpe, applied for a licence to alienate in mortmain a house, land and rent in York, West Cottingwith and Green Hammerton.

We know that Thomas had a sister, Isabella, but it remains to be seen what relation Thomas was to the prioress of Thicket, Alice de Alverthorp, but they were most like close kin, if not another sister of Thomas. The resignation of Alice de Alverthorpe was also recorded in the register of Archbishop Melton, probably due to her old age, in 1335.

Elizabeth de Haye

The nuns of Thicket elected Elizabeth de Haye unanimously as their prioress after the resignation of Alice de Alverthorpe. But the Archbishop ruled the election uncanonical, and quashed the election. But, bearing in mind the unanimity of the election he then appointed Elizabeth de Haye as prioress by his own pontifical authority, and sent a mandate to John Gower, the rector of Wheldrake to install her, dated 2 May 1335. The entry in the Archbishop's register has a memorandum attached to this entry, which states that John Gower, the rector of Wheldrake, did install Elizabeth on the same day.

Elizabeth next occurs in 1337, when Agnes, daughter of James de Lissyngton complained that Elizabeth, Prioress of Thickeheved and others disseised her of houses and land in Sand Hutton. The defenders said that the property was acquired by Joan, the late prioress.

Elizabeth de Haye was still at Thicket in 1345, when she is mentioned in the will of her father, Peter del Hay of Spaldington.

Hawise

Little is known about this prioress. She occurs just once in contemporary records, in 1412, when she was involved in a plea of trespass against John Atkynson.

Alice Darwent

Occurs in 1432 when along with one of her nuns, Agnes Systerannes and a labourer, John Hunt of Cottingwith, they were sued by John Duram for chasing with dogs twelve cows and a hundred sheep, and inciting the dogs to bite them, so that five cows and forty sheep, valued at £7, died, and others much 'deteriorated'.

Interestingly, an Alice Derwent occurs in February 1405/6 when the prior of Ellerton was commissioned by the Dean and Chapter of York, the *see* being vacant at that time, to enclose her, in a house adjoining the conventual church of Thicket. It is unclear if this refers to her as being a nun, and if she was, if this is the same Alice Darwent who became prioress. She may have been enclosed as a punishment, or had chosen to become an anchoress.

Neither the surname Darwent nor Derwent occurs in any of the York Probate Registers, or in any of the Chancery Rolls for this period.

Beatrix

Another prioress about whom very little is known, occurring just once in contemporary records, in 1479, when she is listed among the members of The Guild of Corpus Christi in the City of York.

Maria Dawson

Occurs as a nun at Thicket in April 1474, when she requested a papal dispensation for a defect of birth (being born of an unmarried man and an unmarried woman), that she may be elected to all offices of the order, below that of Abbess, and while still a nun requested a further dispensation in May 1482, for the same reason. She occurs in 1497 as prioress, when she is listed among the members of The Guild of Corpus Christi in the City of York.

Katherine Chapman

Previously a nun of Clementhorpe. The confirmation of Katherine Chapman as prioress of Thykhede occurred on the 23 March, 1525/6. The confirmation reads:

[Marginal Heading] Sentence of confirmation of the election of the Prioress of Thicket.

[Main Text] In the name of God, Amen, The merits and circumstances of the business of the election of you, Lady Katherine Chapman, sister and nun of the nunnery of Saint Clement near the walls of the City of York, elected as prioress of the nunnery of Thicket, of the order of Saint Benedict, in the diocese of York, by the Sub-prioress and convent of the same nunnery of Thicket,

Having been heard, examined, considered and fully discussed by us, Brian Higdon, Doctor of Laws, Dean of the Metropolitan Church of York and Vicar General in Spiritualties of the Most Reverend Father and Lord in Christ, Thomas, by divine mercy Lord Cardinal Priest of the title of Saint Cecilia of the Holy Roman Church, Archbishop of York, and also legate a latere of the Apostolic See, Primate of England, and Chancellor acting in remote parts,

And because, all the proceedings done in the aforementioned matter of the election having been scrutinised and reviewed by us, it stands clear to us, and we have found, by the acts enacted, led out, alleged, propounded, proved, exhibited, produced, testified and acknowledged in the same matter, that the said election was and is evidently canonical, correctly and canonically carried out, and your person fitting and suitable,

For that reason we, Brian Higdon, the beforesaid Dean and Vicar General in Spiritualties, the name of Christ having first been invoked, pronounce, decree and declare that the same election of you, Lady Katherine Chapman, an expressly professed nun of the Order Regular of Saint Benedict, certainly a woman with goodness of habit, knowledge of letters, commendable in merit, being of lawful age and begotten from lawful matrimony, experienced and most circumspect in matters spiritual and temporal, was and is correctly and canonically carried out, and valid and canonical in law,

And by the authority of the said most reverend father we decree that the same election is to be approved and confirmed, and in these writings we do so approve and confirm it, making good defects in the same election, if such there have been, by the same gracious authority.

By these presents, moreover, we commit to you, Lady Katherine Chapman, so elected and confirmed, the care, rule and free administration of both spiritualties and temporalities of the nunnery of Thicket aforesaid, decreeing you into the real and corporal possession of the nunnery of Thicket aforesaid, and of all its rights and appurtenances, actually to be installed in the same place by the Archdeacon of Cleveland or his Official, by induction, as is the custom.

This sentence of the confirmation of the election of Lady Katherine Chapman was read in the consistory of the Metropolitan Church of York,

On Wednesday, that is to say, the 23rd day of the month of March in the year of our Lord, according to the course and computation of the English church, 1525, in the thirteenth pontifical indiction, and in the third year of our most holy father and lord in Christ, our Lord the Pope, Clement the Seventh,

By the aforenamed worshipful Master Brian Higdon, the beforesaid Dean and Vicar General in Spiritualties,

These being then and there present; Master Tristan Teshe, Notary Public, writer of the acts of the said consistory, Sir Edward Midilton, chaplain, William Tyas, learned man, and Master John Chapman, Notary Public, Registrar etc. of the said most reverend father. [End Main Text]

Katherine was mentioned again as the prioress of Thykhede during the *Valor Ecclesiasticus* of 1535, and is listed in the first draft of the Suppression Papers, 15 June 1536. Katherine is also mentioned in a York Account Roll, dated between autumn 1537 and spring 1537/8. However, when the final draft of the Suppression Papers was made, 27 August 1539, Katherine's name is crossed out, and the name of Agnes Beckwith was inserted as prioress instead. It can only be assumed that Katherine Chapman had either resigned or died in the intervening period.

Katherine would only have been aged 51 years in 1539, so did she resign rather than sign the Oath of Supremacy? The fact that she was replaced, not by an existing nun at Thicket, but an outsider, Agnes Beckwith, a nun of Arthington, also gives pause for thought.

Agnes Beckwith
The last prioress of Thicket, who surrendered the priory 27 August 1539, receiving a pension of £6 13s. 4d.

Agnes went on to marry a Gilbert Parr of York, but during the Marian Reaction, when Queen Mary reintroduced Catholicism, the marriage came before the ecclesiastical authorities in York in 1555. Dr. Dakyn, the Official of the Court of Audience in York heard their confession, and imposed a relatively mild penance of fasting and prayer, but also divorced them and commanded them to abstain from cohabiting at once. It is not known if they complied with this order, and with Queen Mary dying in 1558 and the reintroduction of Protestantism by her half-sister, Elizabeth I, the couple would have been free to cohabit once more if they had complied.

Agnes was mentioned in the will of John White of York, a curate of St. Crux, St. Helen on the Walls, and St. Nicholas, and a former keeper of the Guild of Corpus Christi. In his will, dated 18 August 1572, he left a 'silver spoon' to Agnes, the former prioress of Thicket.

Agnes was still alive in 1573 but she had died by 1582.

Prioresses

Period	Name	Source
Occurs 1214–1219	Sybil	Burton's *Monasticon*, pp. 192, 280, quoting Chartulary de Fountains, no. 38, when Sibilla quitclaimed to Fountains the precinct and bailiwick of Wheldrake Castle. A witness was Henry de Redman, Sheriff of York, 1211–1214. Occurs in 1219, *Feet of Fines 1218–1231*, p. 24
Occurs 1231	Eve	Occurs in 1231, *Feet of Fines 1218–1231*, pp. 135–136
Before 1280	Alice	Baildon's *Notes*, p. 45. Prioress Joan, who occurs in 1280, speaks of Alice, the late prioress of Thicket
Occurs 1280–1306	Joan	Burton's, *Monasticon*, pp. 192–280; Baildon's *Notes* vol. 1, (YASRS 17), pp. 208–9. *Feet of Fines for the County of York, from 1272 to 1300*, p.45
1309–1335	Alice de Alverthorpe	Burton's *Monasticon*, p. 281, quoting Reg. William Grenfeld, p. 116, dated 2 Ides (12) of August, 1309. *The Register of William Melton*, vol. 6, no. 652 (p. 211). Memorandum that on 20 April 1335, a letter was sent to the subprioress and convent of Thicket to elect a prioress, vacant by the cession of Alice de Alverthorpe

Occurs 1335	Elizabeth de Haye	Reg. Melton, vol. 6, no. 654 (p. 211). Mandate to rector of Wheldrake to install Elizabeth del Haye, 2 May 1335
Occurs 1412	Hawise	Baildon's *Notes*
Occurs 1432	Alice Darwent	Baildon's *Notes*
Occurs 1479	Beatrix	*The Register of the Guild of Corpus Christi in the City of York*, (Surtees Society, vol. 57), p. 104
Occurs 1497, possibly 1482	Maria Dawson	*The Register of the Guild of Corpus Christi in the City of York*, (Surtees Society, vol. 57), p. 145
1525–1535	Katherine Chapman	Reg. Thomas Wolsey, fol. 82. 23 March, 1525. Also occurs 1535, *Valor Ecclesiasticus*, (Rec. Com.), vol. v, p. 94. Formerly a nun of Saint Clement at York
1539 (Surrender)	Agnes Beckwith, prioress at the Dissolution	Received £6 13s. 4d. (Augmentation Books, vol. 234, p. 268b.) L. and P. Hen. VIII, xv, p. 551

The nuns of Thicket came from a variety of backgrounds and for a variety of reasons. For many young girls a nunnery could have been the only means by which they could gain an education, which may have led some of them to embrace the merits of convent life and become a postulant on completing their studies. Sad to say, some unwanted young girls became oblates, a girl given in childhood to a convent or nunnery by her parents, to be brought up as a nun, typically when a father had some daughters already that he needed to find dowries for, increasing his financial pressures.

In the case of young women for whom marriage was a remote possibility, convent life was often the only alternative available to the family and many fathers found it cheaper to enrol their daughters into a local nunnery, and pay the equivalent of a dowry on entry as a novice. Of course, not all girls went willingly.

For many women the religious life was a genuine calling and the Cult of the Virgin was particularly popular in the medieval period. Entry into a nunnery was also a popular choice for widows. A novice might also be an older lady looking to settle down to a contemplative and secure retirement or wanting to enrol simply to prepare themselves for the next life before time ran out.

The nuns of Thicket lived under the Rule of St. Benedict, but central to the Rule were three basic vows: Obedience, Stability (staying in the house where profession was made) and Conversion of Manners (poverty and chastity).

This kind of life meant that they rarely, if ever, came to the attention of the lay authorities, and consequently very little is known about them. Occasionally they may act as a witness when the prioress defends the priory's rights in a lay court, or when they incur the disapprobation of the ecclesiastical authorities, and occasionally when they rise from the ranks of the sisterhood to be elected as the head of the priory. However, a few nuns of Thicket have been identified:

Lady Elizabeth de Lasceles
Presumably, given that she is described as 'Lady', this was the widow of Roger de Lascelles, lord of Escrick, who died c. 1300. Elizabeth died 1323.

Alice Darel of Wheldrake
On 5 February 1302-3 the archbishop wrote to the prioress and convent respecting Alice Darel, of Wheldrake, an apostate nun of their house, directing that if she returned to them in a contrite spirit they were to impose upon her the penance provided by their rule, but if she did not willingly undergo it, then they were to place her in some secure chamber, under safe custody.

The lordship of Wheldrake belonged to Fountains Abbey at this time, and the Darels were their under-tenants. Alice was apparently an unwilling nun, so was probably a daughter of the under-tenant of Fountains in Wheldrake, but it is unclear which Darel this was. She was possibly the daughter of William Darel, who held one carucate in Wheldrake under Henry de Percy.

Margaret de Langtoft

Margaret was previously a nun in Rosedale Priory, but due to the ravages of the Scots was moved to Thicket in 1332 for protection.

Agnes de Harington

Sent from Nunkeeling to Thicket for penance for her 'rebellion and obstinacy'.

Alice, daughter of Richard Griffoun

Richard Griffoun was a witness in a Proof of Age, for William Gramary, in 1355/6. At the time he said he was 70 years of age, but he remembers in the week that William Gramary was born (November/December 1333), he had a daughter named Alice who was made a nun in the Priory of Thikheved. So Alice's father was about 48 years old when his daughter, Alice, became a nun in 1333.

Joan de Crackenholme

On 26 January 1343-4 Archbishop Zouch wrote to the prioress and convent concerning Joan de Crakenholme, their sister nun, who was coming to them absolved from her crimes of apostasy in frequently leaving the house, laying aside her habit, as well as other excesses which are not stated. For her notorious sins the archbishop had imposed the following, in addition to her private penance. She was not to wear the black veil, or speak to any secular person of either sex, or with her sister nuns, except by leave of the prioress. She was not to go out of the cloister into the church, but was to be confined in a secure place near the church, in such a way, however, that she could be at matins and masses celebrated in the church. She was to do such things as were burdensome and not of honour, attending nevertheless divine service. She was not to dispatch any letter, or receive any sent to her. Each Wednesday and Friday she was to have bread, vegetables and light ale, and was to eat and drink on the bare ground, and on each of those days was to receive a discipline from the prioress and each of the nuns in chapter. She was to take the last place in quire, and not to enter the chapter except to receive her discipline, and was to retire immediately she had received it. Two nuns were to be appointed by the prioress as her guardians, to see to the execution of the archbishop's orders, and the prioress was to have all carried out as a terror to others.

It is one of the most severe punishments visited on any monk or nun recorded in York Registers.

Isabella de Lyndesay

In April 1352 Archbishop Zouche had to write to Thicket Priory again concerning a recalcitrant nun, this time Isabella de Lyndesay, and he enjoined the Prioress to punish her after her faults were uncovered during a recent visitation of the priory by the Archbishop's commissaries. The letter (translated to English) read:

> *William etc, to his beloved daughter the Prioress of the nunnery of Thicket in our diocese, greeting, grace and blessing.*
>
> *Notwithstanding that lately, in the visitation which we made in your said house through our trustworthy commissaries, they had fittingly, lawfully and well-foundedly caused certain acts to be pursued against Isabel de Lyndesey, a fellow nun of your same house, which, in order that we might spare your reputation, we have not thought fit to be inserted into these presents,*
>
> *For which acts indeed, committed by the said Isabel in peril of her soul and contrary to the decency of her order, and confessed before our said commissaries, a certain penance had been imposed and enjoined upon the same Isabel, just as seemed expedient for the health of her soul, and it had been agreed upon by instituted canons,*
>
> *The aforesaid Isabel, however, taking no notice of her oath of obedience, as we take it, refusing now to enter upon the penance thus imposed upon her, led by a spirit of rebellion, does not care nor wish to undergo the discipline of her order, which she is expressly professed to follow, in peril of her soul and to the manifest scandal of the said order, and setting a very bad example to others,*
>
> *Therefore we, who by virtue of the office duly committed to us are bound to call back straying sheep at the outset, like those of a good shepherd, lest the life-blood of those straying, being out of our hands, has to be looked after by a multitude in the end,*

Order you, by virtue of your oath of obedience, firmly enjoining you, more strictly to compel the aforenamed Isabel to undergo and perform the corporal penance imposed upon her, and due according to the rule of your order, and accustomed to be made in similar cases.

You should not neglect certifying to us, before the coming feast of Pentecost, how the said Isabel has conducted herself in this, her penance to be performed, and whether signs of true contrition have appeared in her, since, according to her contrition, or that being absent, her resistance, this penance is worth moderating, or even increasing.

Goodbye. Given at Cawood on the twentieth day of the month of April in the one thousand three hundred and fifty second year of our Lord, and in the tenth year of our episcopacy.

Agnes Systerannes

Almost certainly the surname is not her surname at all, but the name of Sister Anne she took on becoming a nun. Agnes occurs in 1432 when along with her Prioress, Alice Darwent and a labourer, John Hunt of Cottingwith, they were sued by John Duram for chasing with dogs twelve cows and a hundred sheep, and inciting the dogs to bite them, so that five cows and forty sheep, valued at £7, died, and others much 'deteriorated'.

Alice Hadilsay and Alice Broghton

Alice Hadilsay and Alice Broghton were two nuns of Thicket who gave evidence in a Cause in the Ecclesiastical Court of York in 1440/1, when the priory complained that the Prior of Ellerton was unjustly attempting to exact tithes from Thicket, while Thicket claimed to be a Cistercian house, and thus exempt. Alice Hadilsay said she had been a nun for 30 years, and was aged over 40, showing she had become a nun while still very young. Alice Broghton said she had been a nun for 40 years, and was aged 49 years, again showing the very young age at which she became a nun.

Mary Dowson

Sister Mary Dowson, born of an unmarried man and an unmarried woman, requested a dispensation that she may be elected and appointed to all administrations and offices, below the dignity of abbess, notwithstanding her defect of birth. Dated at Rome (St. Peter's), 16 April 1474. Requested a further dispensation from her defect of birth, 9 May 1482.

Nuns identified to the end of the fifteenth century

Year	Name	Source
1301	Commission to the prior of Ellerton to admit the profession of lady Elizabeth de Lasceles 'in domo de Thykheued'	The Register of Thomas of Corbridge, Lord Archbishop of York, 1300–1304, p. 123, dated 22 Apr 1301
1303	Alice Darel of Wheldrake, an apostate	VCH Yorks. III, pp. 124
1322	Margaret de Langtoft, previously at the monastery of Rosedale, moved to Thicket for protection against Scots invaders	Reg. Melton, fol. 240
1325	Agnes de Harington, sent from Nunkeeling Priory to Thicket	Register Melton, vol. 2, nos. 384-5, pp. 114-115
1333	Alice, daughter of Richard Griffoun	CIPM, vol. 10, no. 272
1333/4	Joan de Crackenholme, said to have left her house several times	VCH Yorks. III, pp. 124
1352	Archbishop Zouch had to inflict a correction on a nun of Thicket, for he wrote on 20 April 1352 'to the prioress, to punish Isabella de Lyndesay, a nun whose faults had	VCH Yorks. III, pp. 124

	been recently revealed at a visitation held by his commissaries, and the prioress was to report before Pentecost how she had behaved during the performance of her penance'	
1432	Agnes Systerannes	De Banco, Mich. 11 Hen. VI, m.507a
1440/1	Dame Alice Hadilsay, aged over 40, been a nun there for 30 years	Cause Papers: CP F.221/1
1440/1	Dame Alice Broghton, aged 49, been a nun there for 40 years	Cause Papers: CP F.221/1
1474, 1482	Mary Dowson, requested a dispensation on two occasions	Supplications…Canterbury & York Society (2014), Entries 2306, 2444

The next group of nuns were all those listed in the build up to the Dissolution of the Monasteries by Henry VIII following his break with Rome, and his 'Act of Supremacy' in 1534, severing the church in England from papal authority.

Following the 'Act of Supremacy', Visitors were sent to every religious house in England to survey the assets and value of each house. The resulting reports were termed the *Valor Ecclesiasticus*. This was followed by The Oath of Supremacy which the heads of all religious houses were required to acknowledge, and in 1536 Visitors were sent out again to every religious house to report on compliance, and also report on the moral character of the inmates of each house. Their reports were termed the *Compendium Compertorum*. Unlike some other nunneries in Yorkshire at this time, the Visitors, Richard Layton and Thomas Lee, could find no fault with the nuns of Thicket, and all were described as '*All of good liffyng and conversacion*'.

The Visitors then made a list dated 13 June 28 Hen. VIII (1536) headed by their prioress, Katherine Chapman. Three years later, the list was updated with a new date, 27 August 31 Hen. VIII (1539), with some ages struck out and replaced with ages three years older. Some names were struck out from the first list, showing that some nuns had either died or had left. However, some names had only one age listed, which likely indicates that the clerks doing the updating were unsure if the nuns were still there.

From the following list it is clear that the prioress, Katherine Chapman, and the nun, Isabella Childe, either died or had left the house. As the list has Agnes Beckwith added to the top of the list in a later hand, it suggests that Agnes joined Thicket in the intervening period to be the prioress, rather than being elected from the existing nuns; and Margaret Swale, Isabella Cawton and Elena Fissher all appear to have joined the priory since the first list in 1536, as they are all in a later hand, or perhaps had moved to Thicket from priories that were dissolved in the first wave of dissolutions.

The list drawn up by the Visitors, and the amendments three years later

Name	*Age*
Agnes Beckwith (Prioress, added to the top of the list in a later hand)	46
Katherine Chapman (Prioress, struck out))	48
Isabella Childe (struck out)	60
Alice Yong	63
Margaret Kytchynman (aged 36 struck out)	39
Dorethea Knyght (aged 30 struck out)	32
Elena Sterkee	33
Matilda Chapman	27
Agnes Hunsley	27
Margaret Swale (in a later hand)	28
Isabella Cawton (in a later hand)	40
Elena Fissher (in a later hand)	26

Agnes Beckwith
Still alive in 1573, but died before 1582. See the section on prioresses.

Alice Yong
In the list of pensioners when Thicket was surrendered in 1539, but does not appear in the next pension list of 1553 when she would have been around 77 years old. As she was awarded the second highest pension it is presumed she was the sub-prioress at that time. She certainly was the oldest.

Margaret Kytchynman
In the pension list of 1556, but missing from the list of 1564.

Dorethea Knyght
In the list of nuns during the Compendium Compertorum in 1536, but not in the list of pensioners when Thicket was surrendered in 1539.

Elena Sterkee (Ellen Starkey, Storkey)
Still alive and in the pension list for 1582.

Matilda Chapman
When the Visitors, Layton and Lee, came to Thicket in February 1535/6, they noted that Matilda Chapman sought release 'from the yoke of religion'. However, she was still there in 1539 when the priory was surrendered, and was recorded as still receiving her pension payments in 1582.

Agnes Hunsley
In receipt of her pension up to 1564, but missing from the 1582 pension list.

Margaret (Marjorie) Swale
The only one of the pensioners in the list of 1552/3 stated to have received the monies due to her. She was still alive and in the pension list for 1582.

Isabel Cawton
Was still in receipt of her pension in 1556 and 1564, but was not in the pension list of 1582.

Elena Fisher
In receipt of her pension in 1556, but not listed in the pension list of 1564.

In addition to the nuns of Thicket there were a certain number of lay brothers in the early years of the priory. Lay brothers were those who chose a religious life, but who did not take holy orders. They were pious and hardworking, and normally drawn from the working class, performing manual labour, or had some specific skill needed by a religious house. They would typically perform the heavy manual work, often both in the house and in the fields. Usually joining a religious house in later life, they were termed *conversi*, to distinguish them from the *oblati*. Not all religious houses used lay brothers; some preferred to use hired servants.

The practice of having lay brothers in a nunnery was less than common in the early medieval period. It was frowned upon as time went on and eventually died out.

In the East Riding during the archiepiscopates of Greenfield and Melton, lay brothers were noticed in the Visitation Decrees of Nunkeeling, Thicket and Swine, and in Swine a Brother Thomas was nominated to be the master of the house. However, neither Nunburnholme nor Wilberfoss mention any *conversi*.

Archbishop Greenfield personally visited Thicket Priory, and followed the visitation with the issue of a decree, dated 1 February 1308/9, in which he decreed that no nuns, lay brothers, or inmates were to be received without his special licence. Similarly, Archbishop Melton had Thicket Priory visited by commissaries in 1318/19, and his decree of 1 March 1318/9 forbad the entry of any more nuns or lay brothers, without adequate funds.

No lay brothers are ever named, and it is not known when the practice of their admittance eventually died out in Thicket, but certainly none were listed in the Suppression Papers of 1539, while servants were.

Chaplains

There were never any formal registration processes for chaplains at Thicket, so references to them are scant and only mentioned indirectly, in wills or the occasional corrody:

John Langtoft

In 1438, John Langton, chaplain, requested in his will that he be buried in the Convent of Thikhede.

John Beltonson

In 1491, John Beltonson of Cottingwith, chaplain, requested in his will that he be buried in Thikehede Priory.

Henry Wilkynson

Returned in the clerical subsidy granted in 1523, and collected in 1526/7, on his clear annual stipend of £4. Named by the Visitors in 1536 as holding a corrody there in return for service. Henry deposed that he was above 60 years of age, and had been at Thicket for 30 years.

John Holme

Also listed by the Visitors in 1536, John Holme was described as 'Chaplayne and Confessor there'.

It is remarkable that in such a small house of less than a dozen nuns in 1535, there would be a need for two chaplains. Presumably Henry Wilkynson was the chaplain for the entire priory, while John Holme was the personal chaplain and confessor for the prioress alone.

Number of Nuns, Servants and Boarders

The community at Thicket typically consisted of twelve nuns, including the prioress, and being a poor priory they usually only admitted a new nun following the death of an existing nun. But add to the sisterhood the lay brothers (though no number for them is ever given), a chaplain, boarders and visitors, and the consequent necessity for the cleaning of rooms and latrines, the changing of bedding and laundry, cooking and clearing up, the care of the horses, oxen and pigs, the many agricultural tasks, harvesting, etc., the management of property and collection of rents, etc., the need for servants is obvious, even for a small house of nuns.

The evidence of servants at Thicket is scant, but they are mentioned occasionally. In 1397, the prioress of Thicket sued John, son of Henry Graunger, for forcefully rescuing his cattle which had been impounded by John Kayvill, the servant of the prioress at Benetland, for customs and services due to her.

In 1432, John Duram sued the prioress of Thicket, Agnes Systerannes, her nun, and John Hunt of Cottingwith, labourer, for chasing his cows and sheep at Cottingwith.

In the Survey of Thicket prior to its dissolution in 1539, the servants in the field book are mentioned (no names), but the nunnery servants are named explicitly and were granted rewards: Eleyn Bruce, 5s.; Mawde Bradford, 3s, 4d.; Thomas Hodgeson Cooke, 2s.; Sir John Holme Chaplayn and Confessor there, 5s.

At Thicket Priory in 1309 there were five secular boarders, including Petronilla de Lincoln with her daughter of seventeen years; and three girls—Agnes de Vesey of a similar age, and two young girls, relatives of Mr John de Nassington jun., aged fourteen, and the other aged eleven. Boarders over the age of twelve years were not normally allowed, except by licence of the archbishop, but these boarders were allowed to remain on condition that their maintenance should not burden the convent. The reasons for these boarders were not given, but the three young girls were probably there to be educated, which was a common practice among the nunneries of the period. The mother and daughter is more problematic. They may have been there after paying for a corrody, if the mother was a widow, or was escaping abuse; or the daughter may have been there for education, but needed her mother's support, but this can only be speculation.

In October 1312, the prioress of Thicket was given leave by the archbishop to receive Joan, wife of Walter de Osgodby, until Whit Sunday. Again, the reasons for this can only be speculative. Three years later, in

October 1315, a reason was explicit, when the prioress of Thicket was granted a licence to grant a corrody to Alice of Weighton.

As the visitation decrees to all nunneries in the East Riding in the medieval period contain a clause reminding the prioresses that is forbidden to take in boarders or inmates or to grant corrodies, without a licence, it was presumably a practice that was not uncommon.

External Community

Thicket Priory has been subject to visitation over the course of its existence and beyond. The main visitations were those conducted by the Archbishop of York in his role as the Bishop of York, rather than in his archiepiscopal capacity; the visitations conducted by the commissioners sent by Thomas Cromwell, the vicegerent and vicar-general of Henry III, following the break with Rome; and the later visitations conducted by the heralds to inspect arms in surviving religious houses.

Archbishops' visitation decrees were usually very formulaic, and many of the same articles were sent to other nunneries following visitation and do not imply that any rules were being broken or needed correcting, but simply a reminder of what was expected.

The nuns were required to follow the rule of their order, observe silence, not leave the convent without leave, and then only to visit friends or relatives for a maximum of two weeks, and always in the company of another nun. They were to tend the sick (if they had an infirmary) according to the illness, with a nun best skilled in that illness. No nuns were to be admitted for money, and any repairs that the Visitors noted were to be implemented. All nuns were to be present at service and the kitchen area was to be kept clear of seculars. Accounts were to be submitted to the archbishop's office, and the common seal of the house and all charters were to be kept under lock and key. The prioress should avail herself of the counsel of the other nuns, and no corrodies, pensions, leases or sales of land should be allowed without licence of the archbishop. The sisters and lay brothers should have differing habits, and be kept in separate quarters.

The above articles were typical, so visitation decrees need to be studied carefully to see if any articles were out of the ordinary and only those articles, in addition to the above, or with interesting qualifiers, will be noted below.

The first Archbishop of York, whose register survives, is Walter de Gray (1215-1255), and we know that during his pontificate he was conducting visitations of his diocese. The Bishop of Durham was also conducting visitations around this time, and the practice extended to bishops throughout England and in France.

Walter de Gray's successors as archbishop, Walter Giffard and William Wickwane also conducted visitations, but not of Thicket. It wasn't until the next archbishop, John le Romeyn, that we find the first recorded mention of Thicket Priory concerning visitation, but it was only a notice of an intent to visit, but no result of the visitation is recorded, nor of it ever having happened. The brief pontificate of Henry Newark (1298-1299) also has no mention of Thicket Priory, nor of his successor, Thomas Corbridge (1300-1304).

Archbishop's Visitation of 1308/9

The first visitation for which the result is known occurs during the pontificate of William Greenfield (1306-1315). There is no recording of the intention to visit, but the decree following the visitation is fully recorded, which was dated 1 February 1308/9. The Visitors appointed to conduct the visitation were William de Beverley and Nicholas de Carleton, and their remit was to correct and reform. The decree did not note anything out of the ordinary.

Archbishop's Visitation of 1314/15

On 16 January 1314/15 notice was sent to the prioress and convent of Thicket of an intended visitation, on Monday, the day after the Purification (3 February 1314/15). Following the visitation, conducted by the archbishop himself, the decree was issued on the 6 February.

No nun to leave the enclosure of the priory without the permission of the prioress or sub-prioress. The prioress to live with the convent, and take its advice on business matters. No sister to wear the black veil.

These articles suggest that some nuns had left the confines of the priory without permission, and the prioress wanted to make the Visitors aware of this fact and to remind the nuns that this was forbidden, and the archbishop and his Visitors would be keeping an eye on things. The articles concerning the prioress living 'with' the convent and on 'business matters' suggests that complaints had been made by one or more of the nuns, that the prioress had been living outside of the priory, and that she had made some foolish business decisions. The article on not wearing the black veil is curious, as it was the normal practice in Catholic countries for novice nuns to wear a white veil and for professed nuns who had taken their solemn vows to wear a black veil.

Shortly after the decree, on 7 March, in what looks like a separate incident, a commission was issued to Master J. Gower, the rector of Wheldrake, to absolve the nuns, sisters and lay brothers of Thicket from the laying of violent hands upon each other, which did not draw blood (one wonders what the fracas was all about), and from admitting nuns upon payment of money.

In the following October of 1315 the archbishop granted a licence to the prioress and convent of Thicket to grant a corrody to Alice of Weighton.

Archbishop's Visitation of 1319/20

A mandate was sent to the prioress and convent of Thicket to attend the archbishop's visitation of their house, (not at their house, but in the cathedral), dated 14 February 1319/20. However, this was superseded by a commission issued on 18 February to the rectors of Brandesburton and Hemsworth, to visit the nunneries of Thicket and Arthington. Following the visitation in late February the archbishop issued his decree on 1 March.

Article (10) in this visitation is noteworthy, in that it enjoined the prioress, under permitted penalties, to love and cherish her fellow nuns. Article (11) is also unusual in that it is emphasised, under penalty of removal from office and excommunication, to desist from charging for services and duties which they should provide as of right. Following the articles the visitors wrote that these were 'beneficial' warnings.

Archbishop's Visitation of 1332

A citation for the visitation of Thicket was sent out 3 April 1332, and the visitation occurred on Tuesday, 29 April. Unfortunately no resulting decree is recorded in the archbishop's register.

Archbishop's Visitation of 1352

Thicket was once again visited in late March 1352, and on this occasion a rebellious nun was found by the commissaries. It was serious enough (but so serious the archbishop would not put it in writing) for the archbishop to write to the prioress to inflict upon the nun a punishment, as penance. The letter reads:

Letters to enforce [one] of the nuns to perform the penance enjoined upon her for certain acts discovered in the visitation by the commissaries

William etc., to his beloved daughter the Prioress of the nunnery of Thicket in our diocese, greeting, grace and blessing.

Notwithstanding that lately, in the visitation which we made in your said house through our trustworthy commissaries, they had fittingly, lawfully and well-foundedly caused certain acts to be pursued against Isabel de Lyndesey, a fellow nun of your same house, which, in order that we might spare your reputation, we have not thought fit to be inserted into these presents,

For which acts indeed, committed by the said Isabel in peril of her soul and contrary to the decency of her order, and confessed before our said commissaries, a certain penance had been imposed and enjoined upon the same Isabel, just as seemed expedient for the health of her soul, and it had been agreed upon by instituted canons,

The aforesaid Isabel, however, taking no notice of her oath of obedience, as we take it, refusing now to enter upon the penance thus imposed upon her, led by a spirit of rebellion, does not care nor wish to undergo the discipline of her order, which she is expressly professed to follow, in peril of her soul and to the manifest scandal of the said order, and setting a very bad example to others,

Therefore we, who by virtue of the office duly committed to us are bound to call back straying sheep at the outset, like those of a good shepherd, lest the life-blood of those straying, being out of our hands, has to be looked after by a multitude in the end,

Order you, by virtue of your oath of obedience, firmly enjoining you, more strictly to compel the aforenamed Isabel to undergo and perform the corporal penance imposed upon her, and due according to the rule of your order, and accustomed to be made in similar cases.

You should not neglect certifying to us, before the coming feast of Pentecost, how the said Isabel has conducted herself in this, her penance to be performed, and whether signs of true contrition have appeared in her, since, according to her contrition, or that being absent, her resistance, this penance is worth moderating, or even increasing.

Goodbye. Given at Cawood on the twentieth day of the month of April in the one thousand three hundred and fifty second year of our Lord, and in the tenth year of our episcopacy.

Isabel's 'crimes' are not mentioned, but previously, Archbishop Zouche had written to the prioress in 1343/4 about another recalcitrant nun, Joan de Crackenholme, who had committed apostasy by frequently leaving the house, without her habit, and other 'excesses'. The archbishop laid down one of the most severe punishments ever laid down for any monk or nun recorded in the York Registers.

The registers of the Archbishops of York from 1352 to the Dissolution of Thicket in 1539 have not been published, with the exception of the pontificates of Robert Waldby (1397), Richard Scrope (1398–1405), and part of the register of Thomas Rotherham (1480–1500). Unfortunately, none of these registers contain any visitation material for Thicket.

The two main visitations of Thicket undertaken by agents of Thomas Cromwell, the vicegerent and vicar-general of Henry VIII following the break from Rome, were the so-called *Compendium Compertorum*, and the follow-up visitation where the Visitors attempted to persuade the prioress of Thicket to surrender the priory, and offering pensions if the prioress and convent agreed. Both visitations were in 1536.

Vicegerent Visitations of 1536

The *Compendium Compertorum* had none of the licentious allegations against Thicket that many other religious houses had levelled against them, the only comment being that one nun, Matilda Chapman, wished to leave.

When the Visitors drew up their first list of the prioress and nuns of Thicket later in 1536 with the proposed pension amounts by their names, the list was headed by the brief comment '*All of Good Lyffing and Conversacion*'.

From the early sixteenth to the late seventeenth centuries the heralds carried out visitations, county by county, in order to regulate the use of arms, and who was allowed to bear them. Yorkshire was visited several times during this period, and occasionally churches and the remains of dissolved religious houses were visited to see what arms were depicted in the stained glass windows and in memorials and brasses etc. One of the most comprehensive exercises conducted by the heralds was the visitation of 1584.

Heraldic Visitation of 1584

The visitation undertaken by Robert Glover, Somerset Herald, in 1584, is unique in all the printed visitations by the heralds in that it included all the arms noted by Glover in the houses of the gentry in Yorkshire, and in the churches and remains of dissolved religious houses.

Unfortunately, no arms were found in Thicket Priory, unlike nearby Ellerton Priory, a priory of Gilbertine monks, just across the River Derwent, which had many examples of heraldic arms in the windows of the church of the priory which had been retained as a parish church. The arms were those of the benefactors of Ellerton Priory, and have survived today, largely intact, and can now be seen in the window facing the north aisle of Selby Abbey, where they were removed to in 1984 prior to the rebuilding of Ellerton Priory Church (but never returned).

Ellerton Priory was founded c. 1207 by William, son of Peter, who was closely connected to the Hay family, the patrons of Thicket Priory, who also became the patrons of Ellerton Priory.

Ellerton Priory was the closest religious house to Thicket, being just two miles south of Thicket, on the other side of the River Derwent, but easily reachable via the ferry at Bubwith, which is known to have existed from at least the twelfth century, and perhaps even nearer at East Cottingwith.

Shortly following the foundation of Ellerton Priory, their patrons, the del Hay family, granted the church of the neighbouring parish of Aughton. The parish of Aughton had two chapelries, East Cottingwith, and Thorganby on the other side of the River Derwent, upon which stood Thicket Priory.

Thus, through proximity, patronage and ecclesiastical ties, the two priories were closely linked. However, although the two priories were physically near each other, their status and influence were miles apart. Ellerton was well endowed and much more prosperous than Thicket, and in the eleventh and twelfth centuries monasteries vastly outnumbered nunneries, not only in England, but throughout Europe. As Janet Burton in her book on the Yorkshire Nunneries pointed out, this state of affairs 'reflected a society in which the male element was dominant, in which endowments for religious houses were for the most part provided by men who accordingly founded monasteries for political and social reasons, as well as from a certain prejudice against women in the religious life. This was manifest not so much in a belief that women could not, or should not lead their lives in religious communities, which indeed they had done since the very early days of the Christian church, but rather in the attitude that their prayers were somehow less effective than those of men'. It is somewhat telling, that by the time of the Dissolution of the Monasteries, not one nunnery in Yorkshire came above the £200 clear annual value to escape the first Dissolution Act.

The first recorded interaction between the two priories came in 1282, when Joan, the prioress of Thicket, sued Adam, the prior of Ellerton, to permit her to have common of pasture in West Cottingwith which belonged to her free tenement there, and of which Henry, the late prior of Ellerton had unjustly disseised Alice, the late prioress of Thicket.

In the early 1400s more serious tensions began to arise between the two priories when the prior of Ellerton began to claim tithes from Thicket, which in 1441 led to a tuitorial appeal being filed in the Ecclesiastical Court of York. Thicket was claiming that it was a Cistercian house, and therefore exempt from tithes, while Ellerton was claiming that Thicket was a Benedictine house and therefore subject to tithes. Fortunately, several of the Cause Papers concerning this case have survived, including notarial instruments authenticating the appeal by Thomas Fosseton, one of the proctors for Thicket, who outlined the case for Thicket in the Positions:

> *In the name of God, Amen, Before you, O Lord Official of the Court of York, or your Commissary General, or another competent judge, the proctor of the religious women the Prioress and Convent of the house or priory of nuns of Thicket, of the Cistercian order or the rule of Saint Benedict, in the diocese of York, in the name of his procuracy for the same, says and proposes in law, [against the religious] men the Prior and Convent of Ellerton, of the order of Saint Gilbert, in the said diocese, and against anyone at all appearing lawfully for the same before you for judgment, and against all and singular others having or who can have an interest in the matter of the underwritten appeal for protection, lawfully interposed at the said Court of York,*

That it is lawful for the aforenamed ladies, the Prioress and Convent of Thicket, who had been and were of good fame, honest conversation, unimpaired opinion and full estate, and free from all reproach, to be freed of and totally immune from payment of whatsoever tithes arising from lands, places and newly tilled land, cultivated by their own labours or hands, or at their own costs, or from foodstuffs of their animals,

And to be in possession of the abovesaid immunity, and of all and singular temporalities and spiritualities annexed to the said priory of Thicket and appertaining to the same ladies in any way whatsoever, and of all tithes of their lands etc above mentioned, according to the exigency of the common law and the privileges of the Holy Roman Fathers and Pontiffs granted to them by the generosity of Kings,

And to be in possession, or rather for these fruits and foodstuffs of their animals, and of sheaves and hay cultivated and nourished at their own costs or by their own labour as is aforesaid, to be had and received, without payment of tithes of the same.

And they shall possess them canonically, and they shall effectively pursue all and singular the things set out before,

Peacefully and quietly reassuring, supporting and approving all and singular those having an interest in this regard, and especially the Prior and Convent of Ellerton aforesaid, saving the things to be said below.

And albeit also, on the part of the said ladies, that they are well known to be in possession or the equivalent of all and singular the premises, they are anxious about the premises, or any of them, from certain probable and credible causes gravely anticipated by them to be possible, or at least in fact for some prejudice to be created in the future,

If anyone at all, by any authority, in anyone's name or place or by their order, should unduly attempt anything contrary to the premises, or any of them, or should cause anything in any way to be attempted, it shall and may be appealed directly to the Holy Apostolic See, and come to the Court of York for protection, openly and publicly summoned and to be summoned.

Moreover, the aforenamed Prior and Convent of Ellerton, well known to be aware of all and singular the premises, and after, contrary to and notwithstanding [the appeal and summons], have unduly molested, disquieted and disturbed the aforenamed ladies being in possession of all the premises, or have ordered, caused and threatened them to be molested, disquieted and disturbed concerning the tithes of all sheaves and hay arising from lands [cultivated] by their labours and at their costs, as is aforesaid, and they do at present so order, cause and threaten them, many times and unjustly,

And they did and do inconsiderately and heedlessly impede those ladies in their possession of these fruits of their labours according to the exigency of the common law and of their abovesaid privileges and indults, [not allowing them] to enjoy, to freely dispose of the same, and to receive and be able to have the same, as they ought, and they did and do have this molestation, disquieting, threatening, impedence and disturbance done, approved and, equally, accepted, in their name, concerning misappropriating these their fruits, unduly threatening them with harm in law, and the prejudice and oppression of those ladies, heedlessly offending against sentences and censures of the said Roman Fathers the Pontiffs solemnly carried out against delinquents in this regard.

Whereupon on behalf of the said religious ladies, perceiving themselves and their aforesaid conventual house to be unduly burdened by the oppressive premises, from all and singular the same oppressions, and from each of them, and on account thereof, and of each of them, and which can be recollected by them and by each of them, there is an appeal for protection in this regard directly to the Holy Apostolic See, and it comes to the abovesaid Court of York, and it is lawful.

Which things were and are true, public, well known and manifest in the city and diocese of York, and in neighbouring places, and by the aforenamed Prior and Convent of Ellerton, and sufficiently acknowledged by their party [representing them] in the presence of the other party, from certain causes and knowledge,

And there was and is public voice and fame concerning these things.

For which reason the said proctor, in the name which is above, seeks that those things in this regard which were to be proved may be sufficiently proved in this regard for the aforesaid Prioress and Convent of Thicket, and he in their name, to be decreed to be protected, with effect, and the benefit of this protection to be granted to the same ladies and their proctor in their name according to the protective quality and nature of this matter, and the laudable customs and statutes of the said court to be observed in these premises by you, the Lord Official or your Commissary or other competent Judge abovesaid in this case,

And indeed that all and singular these oppressions, attempted after and contrary to the summons and appeal abovesaid, to the prejudice of the aforenamed ladies and their house and the party [representing them], in general, and in so far as it is possible to be clear concerning them, in particular, be revoked and duly reserved according to the laudable customs and statutes of the said court, and further for that which is just to be done for him in the premises, and in anything concerning them, according to the nature and quality of the same in all things.

The said proctor, in the name which is above, says and seeks, and intends to prove, these things, and he himself offers such things, jointly and severally, to be proved as are sufficient for it in this regard, always saving the benefit of law.

Thicket produced several witnesses to testify, by written deposition, that Ellerton had indeed been attempting to force the payment of tithes from Thicket, and depositions were brought before the court by two of the nuns of Thicket:

Dame Alice Hadilsay, aged over forty, deposed that she had been a professed nun there for 30 years, and further deposed that in autumn of the previous year she had been in the church of Thicket when the prior of Ellerton with his men had appeared in person to demand the prioress pay tithes before the removal of any hay, sheaves of corn, or any other harvest from lands within the parish of Aughton, the church of which belonged to Ellerton, and that later on the same day, she was in the hall of the prioress when two canons of Ellerton, with the authority of the church of York, forbade the removal of hay from the nunnery lands of Aughton.

Dame Margaret Broghton, aged 49 years, and a nun for 40 years (*sic*), gave a similar deposition.

Further depositions were given by local people:

Robert Barker, aged 53 years, of Wheldrake, deposed that he had been born in the parish of Wheldrake, close to Thicket Priory, which had several pieces of arable land and seven acres of meadow, and throughout his lifetime had cultivated these at their own expense. He had seen their servants take away sheaves and hay, without any payment of tithe. This had been done from time out of mind and was openly believed by the people of Wheldrake. It was, he claimed, six years ago that the canons of Ellerton had first unjustly taken tithes from certain lands. He was not able to depose on the second position, but on the third he had heard tell that the prior had, the previous autumn, gone with one of his canons to the house of Thicket and had threatened the nuns. He was also unable to comment on the fourth point, but on the final article he confirmed that all the matters were indeed well known in Wheldrake.

Nicholas Darrel, aged 67 years, of West Cottingwith (which he stated to be half a mile from the nunnery), attested in much the same manner. However, he claimed that it was fourteen years ago when the prior and certain canons of Ellerton had taken tithes of sheaves and wheat from a certain close or lands, called vulgariter 'intake', and carried them off on their shoulders. He attested that the previous autumn the prior of Ellerton had gone to the conventual church of Thicket and had forbidden the nuns to remove hay, sheaves, or harvest from their lands and meadows. The witness, Nicholas, saw this as, he claims, did John Stillingfleet, William Grayve, John Lange the younger, and Robert Hueson of Cottingwith.

Henry Qweldryke of Thorganby, of the age of 60 years and more, a witness admitted, sworn, and diligently examined upon the libel annexed to these presents,

Examined and questioned upon the first particular, he says he believes this particular to contain the truth,

Because he says that he has had notice for the 40 years last past that the priory or house of nuns of Thicket, which priory of house the libel concerns, and because, as he says, for all those years he has made his home continuously in the town of Thorganby, distant by the space of half a mile, as it were, from the same conventual house, and so far as he ever knew or understood, up to the time the present dispute was moved, as he says, the prioress and convent of the aforesaid house or priory, were and are totally free and immune from all and all manner of payment of any tithe of sheaves and hay from their own lands and meadows occupied and cultivated at their own costs, or arising from foodstuffs of any of their animals whatsoever,

And moreover he says he has often heard it said that five or six years ago the Prior and Convent of Ellerton disturbed the aforesaid religious women, in possession of the premises to the extent that they carried and moved away the tenth parts of sheaves arising from certain lands of the aforesaid nuns, cultivated at their own costs in their cells, to other remote places, and disposed of the same as it pleased them,

And [they did] this unjustly as he believes just as he, having been sworn, believes, as according to the belief of this sworn man, as he says.

And otherwise, having been examined, he says he knows not how to depone upon this particular.

Examined and questioned upon the 2nd particular, he knows not how to depone, as he says.

Upon the 3rd and 4th particulars, he says he knows not how to depone, except from the statement from what he has heard of others.

Examined upon the 4th last particular, he says that the premises deponed by him were and are public, well-known and open matters in the aforesaid town of Thorganby and other towns surrounding it, and the public voice and fame in the same place laboured for a long time, and still do labour, upon the same.

And he has not been led, instructed, bribed or incited to depone just as he has above deponed, as he says on his oath.

The cause papers also contained the appointment of the proctor for Ellerton, and the proctors for Thicket, Robert Chigwall, William Byspham, John Saxton and Thomas Fosseton, and in addition to the depositions the Positions document contains on the dorse, the names of the deponents, plus three other names: Thomas Barnebe of Topcliffe; Robert Hudeson of Thorganby; and William Skelton of Thorganby.

But the key document for Thicket was a Papal Bull of Pope Gregory IX, dated at Rieti, 8 May 1228, which provided the evidence for their exemption from tithes:

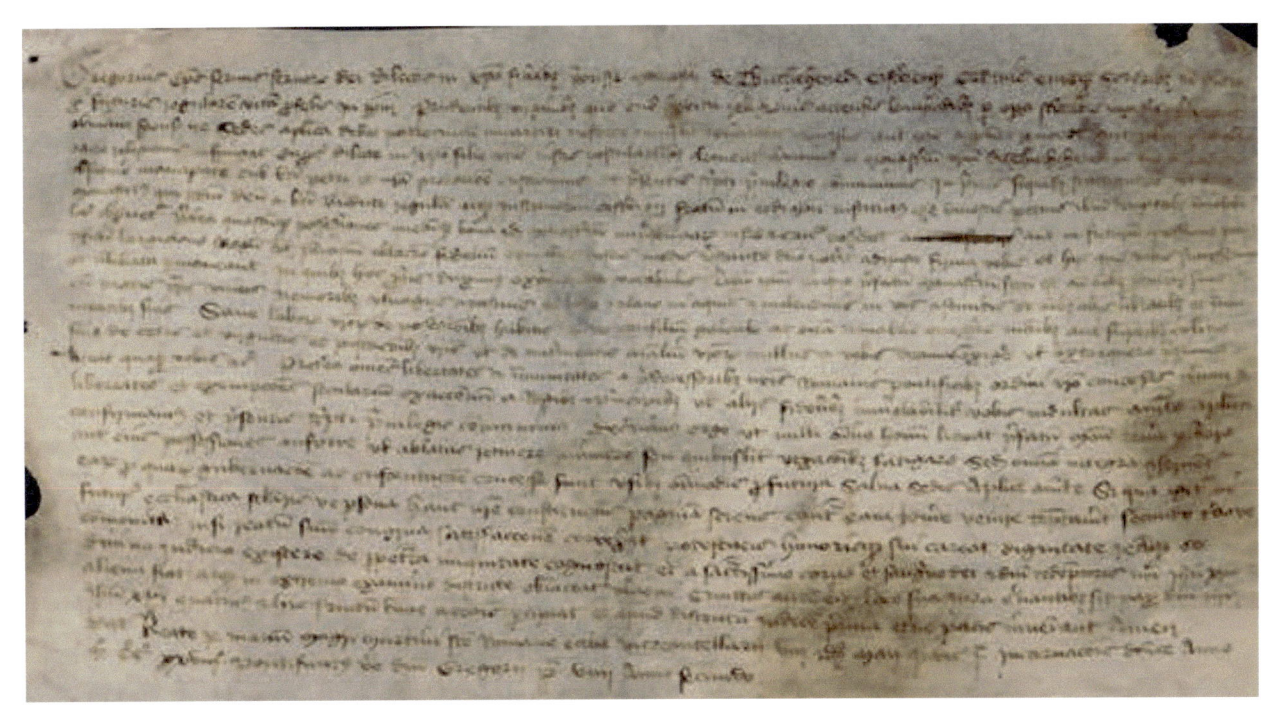

Papal Bull of Pope Gregory IX

The Papal Bull is in remarkably good condition considering its age, and ultra-violet light brings out the faded text. The scribes who wrote out the Bull used medieval ecclesiastical Latin in a highly abbreviated form. A full transcription of the Bull now follows, with the expansion of the abbreviated words shown in square brackets.

Papal Bull of Pope Gregory IX
(Transcription, Latin)

Gregorius Ep[iscopus] servus servor[um] dei dilectis in χρ[ιστ]o filiab[us] P[ri]orisse Monast[er]ii de Thiccheheved Cist[er]ciens[is] Ordinis eiusq[ue] Sororib[us] t[a]m p[rese]ntibus q[ua]m futur[is] regulare[m] vita[m] p[ro]fessis In p[er]p[et]u[um] Prudentib[us] virginib[us] que sub habitu religionis accensis lampadib[us] p[er] op[er]a s[an]c[ti]tatis iugit[er] se p[re]parant obviam sponso ire

Sedes Ap[osto]lica debet patrociniu[m] impartiri ne forte cuiusli[be]t tem[er]itatis incursus aut eas a p[ro]po[s]ito revocet aut robur quod absit sacre religionis infringat

Eap[ro]pt[er] dilecte in χρ[ιστ]o filie v[est]ris iustis postulac[i]o[n]ib[us] clement[er] a[n]nuim[us] et Monast[er]iu[m] v[est]r[u]m de Thiccheheved in quo divino estis obsequio mancipate sub b[ea]ti petri et n[ost]ra protecc[i]o[n]e suscipimus et p[re]sentis sc[ri]pti p[ri]vilegio co[m]munimus

In p[ri]mis siquid[em] statuentes ut ordo Monastic[us] qui s[e]c[un]d[u]m deu[m] et b[ea]ti B[e]n[e]dicti regula[m] atq[ue] Instituc[i]o[ne]m Cist[er]cien[sium] fratru[m] in eod[em] Mon[asterio] institut[us] esse dinoscit[ur] p[er]petuis ib[ide]m temporib[us] i[n]violabilit[er] obs[er]vet[ur]

P[re]t[er]ea quascu[n]q[ue] possessiones quecu[n]q[ue] bona id[em] Monast[er]iu[m] imp[re]senciar[um] iuste et can[oni]ce possidet aut in futuru[m] [con]cessione pontificu[m] largicione Regu[m] v[el] p[ri]ncipiu[m] oblac[i]o[n]e fideliu[m] seu aliis iustis modis p[re]stante d[omi]no pot[er]it adipisci firma vobis et hiis que vobis successerint et illibata p[er]maneant

In quib[us] hec p[ro]p[ri]is duxim[us] exp[ri]menda vocabulis locu[m] ip[su]m in quo p[re]fatu[m] Monast[er]iu[m] situ[m] est cu[m] o[mn]ib[us] p[er]tinen[ciis] suis cu[m] pratis t[er]ris vineis nemorib[us] ulnagiis et pascuis in bosco et plano in aquis et molendinis in viis et semitis et o[mn]ib[us] aliis lib[er]tatib[us] et i[m]munitatib[us] suis

Sane labor[um] v[est]ror[um] de possessio[n]ib[us] habitis ante consiliu[m] gen[er]ale ac ecia[m] novaliu[m] quo p[ro]p[ri]is ma[n]ib[us] aut su[m]ptib[us] colitis sive de ortis et virgultis et piscac[i]o[n]ib[us] v[est]ris v[e]l de nut[ri]mentis a[n]i[m]aliu[m] v[est]ror[um] nullus a vobis decimas exig[er]e v[e]l extorquere p[re]sumat

Liceat quoque vobis &c

P[re]t[er]ea om[n]es libertates et i[m]munitates a p[re]decessorib[us] n[ost]ris Romanis Pontificib[us] ordini v[est]ro concessas n[ec]non et libertates et exempc[i]o[n]es secular[u]m exacc[i]onu[m] a Regib[us] et p[ri]ncipib[us] v[e]l aliis fidelib[us] inviolabilit[er] vobis indultas auc[torita]te ap[osto]lica confirmam[us] et p[re]sentis sc[ri]pti p[ri]vilegio co[m]munim[us]

Dec[er]nim[us] ergo ut nulli o[mn]ino homi[num] liceat p[re]fatu[m] Mon[asterium] tem[er]e p[er]t[ur]bare aut eius possessiones auferre v[e]l ablatas retinere minuere seu quibusli[be]t vexac[i]o[n]ib[us] fatigare

Sed om[n]ia integra [con]serve[n]t[ur] ear[um] p[ro] quar[um] gubernac[i]o[n]e ac sustentac[i]o[n]e concessa sunt usib[us] o[mn]imodis p[ro]futura Salva Sedis Ap[osto]lice auc[torita]te

Si qua igit[ur] in futur[um] eccl[es]iastica s[e]c[u]laris ve p[er]sona hanc n[ost]re constituc[i]o[n]is pagina[m] sciens cont[ra] eam tem[er]e venire te[m]ptav[er]it secundo t[er]ciove co[m]monita: nisi reatu[m] suu[m] congrua satisfacc[i]one correx[er]it potestatis honorisq[ue] sui careat dignitate rea[m]q[ue] se divino judicio existere de p[er]pet[ra]ta iniquitate cognoscat et a sac[ra]tissimo corp[or]e et sang[ui]ne dei et d[omi]ni rede[m]ptoris n[ost]ri Jh[es]u χρ[ιστ]ι aliena fiat atq[ue] in extremo examine districte s[u]biaceat ultioni

Cunctis aute[m] eid[em] loco sua iura s[er]vantib[us] sit pax d[omi]ni n[ost]ri Jh[es]u χρ[ιστ]ι quatin[us] et hic fructu[m] bone acc[i]o[n]is p[er]cipia[n]t et apud districtu[m] iudice[m] p[re]mia et[er]ne pacis inve[n]iant Amen

Dat[um] Reate p[er] manu[m] Mag[ist]ri Martini s[an]c[t]e Romane eccl[es]ie vicecancellarii viij id[us] Maii Indic[cione] ja Incarnac[i]o[n]is d[omi]nice Anno Mo CCo xxviijo Pontificat[us] v[er]o d[omi]ni Gregorii P[a]p[e] viiij Anno secundo

Papal Bull of Pope Gregory IX
(Translation, English)

Bishop Gregory, servant of the servants of God, to his beloved daughters in Christ, the Prioress of the Monastery of Thicket, of the Cistercian order, and her sisters, both present and future, prudent maidens professed to a life according to rule in perpetuity, who in the habit of religion, with torches lit by works of holiness, prepare themselves jointly to go by way of one betrothed.

The Apostolic See owes protection to be bestowed lest by chance an effort of any temerity whatsoever may either recall them from that purpose or, sacred religion being absent, may weaken a stronghold.

For that reason we acknowledge to our beloved daughter in Christ that we have kindly assented to your just requests, and to those of your Monastery of Thicket, in which you are entitled to perform divine service under the protection of the Blessed Peter and ourselves, and by the privilege of this present writing we reinforce,

Establishing in the first place, since it is decreed that the monastic order which follows God and the rule of the Blessed Benedict and the institution of Cistercian Brothers is to be instituted in the same monastery, it shall be inviolably observed in the same place for all time in perpetuity.

Moreover, whatsoever possessions and goods the same monastery may possess, justly and canonically, at the present time or in the future, by the grant of pontiffs, the generosity of kings or princes, the oblation of the faithful, or by any just means, serving the Lord, may be retained by it, and they may remain, firm and unimpaired, with you and those who succeed you,

Among which we have decided to express these things in our own words; the place itself in which the aforenamed monastery is sited, with all its appurtenances, with its meadows, lands, vineyards, woodlands, wineries and feedings, its woods and open places, its waters and mills, its roads and footpaths, and all its other liberties and immunities;

Indeed, none should presume to exact or extort tithes from you, from possessions of your labours had before this general advice, and also of newly tilled land which was cultivated by your own hands, or at your own costs, or from your gardens, copses and fisheries, or from foodstuffs of your animals.

Also it may be lawful for you etc.

Moreover we confirm, and by the privilege of this present writing reinforce, all liberties and immunities granted to your order by our predecessor Roman Pontiffs, and indeed liberties and exemptions from secular exactions granted by kings and princes, or by other faithful people, inviolably to you, and indults granted by Apostolic authority.

We therefore decree that to no man at all shall it be lawful heedlessly to disturb the aforenamed monastery, or carry away its possessions, or to retain any so carried away, or to weary or harass it with any vexations whatsoever,

But all of those things should be preserved entire, for the governance and sustenance of those to whom they were granted, to all manner of uses for the future, saving the authority of the Apostolic See,

If therefore any person in the future, ecclesiastical or secular, knowing of this deed of our constitution, having been warned, shall heedlessly attempt to go against it for a second or third time, unless he shall have corrected his guilt with fitting satisfaction, let him lose the dignity of his power and honour, and know that he is subject to divine justice; let him acknowledge the injury perpetrated, and let him be estranged from the most sacred body and blood of God and our Lord and redeemer Jesus Christ; and in the final judgment let him undergo severe vengeance.

Moreover, for all those preserving their rights in the same place, may there be the peace of our Lord Jesus Christ, so that they may here receive the fruit of their good deed, and before their righteous judge find the reward of eternal peace, Amen.

Given at Rieti by the hand of Master Martin, Vicechancellor of the Holy Roman Church, on the 8th ides of May, in the 1st indiction, in the 1228th year of the dominical incarnation, and indeed in the second year of the pontificate of our Lord Pope Gregory IX.

Unfortunately, there is no record of the outcome of this dispute, although in all subsequent correspondence between the Archbishop of York and Thicket, the archbishop always refers to them as being of the 'order' of St. Benedict, though that alone does not preclude Thicket from having won their case.

The people that Thicket Priory came into contact with the most were the local people of West Cottingwith, Thorganby and Wheldrake, who were primarily involved in agriculture, mainly as agricultural labourers, some of whom would have worked for the nuns on their demesne lands. Others, further up the social scale, would have been tenants of the nuns on their other land holdings, or as agents of Thicket for those holdings. Unfortunately, the names of the labourers working for the nuns, or the agents, are seldom recorded, and those that were have already been identified in the Servants sub-section of the Internal Community Section.

Occasionally, the nuns would come into contact with local merchants in their parler, where they could buy provisions and other needed goods, or sell their ale, wool, and other produce from their demesne lands that were surplus to requirements, but no names have been forthcoming.

The only local people that were named from time to time were the families from the upper end of the social spectrum. This included the patrons of Thicket Priory, which as we have seen in the Foundation and Endowments Section, were the descendants of the founders, the 'de' Haye family of Aughton; and other local lords. In the lay subsidy of 1301 for the vill of Wheldrake, two local lords are named: Magistro Joanne de Craucumbe, who was assessed at 31s. 6d.; Willelmo Darell, assessed at 8s. 10d.; and the Priorissa de Thickeved, assessed at 9s. 10d. It is interesting that the prioress (or priory) is not assessed in the lists for Thorganby or West Cottingwith, which would appear that, for tax purposes, the domicile of Thicket was regarded as Wheldrake.

The manor of Aughton continued in the Haye family until the end of the fourteenth century, when German Haye married Alice de Aske, daughter of John de Aske and Joan de Shelvestrode. German died without issue and Alice, his widow, remarried a Thomas Miton (Myton). By some mechanism the manor of Aughton was carried by Alice to her new husband, Thomas Myton. This is unusual, as normally if German had died without issue it would have descended to another in the male line of the Hayes, rather than be carried out of the family on remarriage. Certainly the Haye family felt aggrieved, and Roger Haye petitioned the king:

'Roger Hay states that he was seised of the manors of Aughton and Everthorpe in Yorkshire in his demesne as in fee, until Alice, widow of Thomas Myton, disseised him through the maintenance of her brother, John Ask. He asks the king to order Alice to come before him to be examined on this, and that he might be restored to possession of his manors.'

The National Archives states that this petition is roughly datable to c. 1380x1415 by the hand, but is certainly later, as in both 1406 and 1420 the manor was described as belonging to Thomas Myton.

The petition was successful in that it resulted in a legal case being brought in Chancery, Rex v. Milton, in 1434.

It would appear that this suit was unsuccessful, as following Alice's death in 1440 we find John Aske's son, Richard Aske, in possession of the manor. John Aske died 2 June 1429. His son and heir, Richard Aske, was aged 10 and over at his father's death.

In 1531 Sir Robert Aske died, and in his *Inquisition Post Mortem* (IPM) he is stated to hold the Manor of Aughton, the patronage of Ellerton Priory, land and rent in West Cottingwith, Bellasize, Bennetland, and in several other places. His son and heir was John Aske, aged over 30 years. The IPM also recited grants to his second son, Christopher Aske.

Sir Robert had three sons and four daughters, John and Christopher were two of the sons, mentioned in the IPM, and the third and youngest was Robert Aske, leader of the famous Pilgrimage of Grace. Following Robert's execution for his part in the insurrection in July 1537, and the completion of the Dissolution of the Monasteries in 1539, the eldest brother, John, did very well out of the whole affair, acquiring the site and lands of the priories of Marrick, Thicket and Ellerton, in fee, in 1542, in exchange for his manors and land in Sussex.

Throughout all this period, from the marriage of German Haye to Alice de Aske at the end of the fourteenth century to the dissolution of Thicket Priory, the Aske family had been the patrons of Thicket Priory, but just how much of the repairs, improvements and enlargements of the site of the priory the Aske family paid for are simply not recorded.

Dissolution

In England, from 1337 to 1453, many religious houses had already begun a process akin to dissolution due to the Hundred Years War, when so-called alien priories, i.e. monasteries and priories in England, but under a mother house typically in France, were suppressed and their assets sequestrated, to prevent money going overseas. The assets and income of these alien priories went directly to the crown instead, and some were transferred to royal supporters, and some were earmarked for educational uses.

Towards the end of the fifteenth century many bishops were advocating more dissolutions, with the estates and assets being used to fund educational foundations, typically in new colleges in Oxford and Cambridge.

The power and wealth of the greater monasteries, and their propensity to litigate, even among the lesser religious houses, caused a great deal of animosity among the laity in medieval England. A renowned theologian and critic of monasticism, Desiderius Erasmus of Rotterdam, 1466–1536, regularly satirised monasteries as lax, as comfortably worldly, as wasteful of scarce resources and as superstitious. He also advocated that monks and nuns should be brought more directly under episcopal authority.

In Germany in 1521, Martin Luther had published *De Votis Monasticis* (Concerning Monastic Vows), which ventured that monastic life had no basis in scripture, had no useful purpose, and was incompatible with the true essence of Christianity; while in Sweden, Denmark and Switzerland, confiscations of monasteries were gaining pace in the late 1520s, with the spread of Lutheranism.

Back in England, Henry VIII failed in his bid of 1527 to get a declaration of nullity from the Pope regarding his childless marriage to Catherine of Aragon, his brother's widow, and in 1531 had himself declared Supreme Head of the Church of England, and began a series of legislation to firmly establish his Supremacy.

Late in 1532 Henry secretly married Anne Boleyn, which was considered unlawful at that time, followed by a second formal wedding service in London on 25 January 1533. Following the death of Archbishop Warhem, Anne proposed Thomas Cranmer as the new Archbishop of Canterbury who was consecrated 30 March 1533. Less than two months later, Cranmer declared the marriage of Henry and Catherine null and void, and five days later, declared the marriage of Henry and Anne valid.

In November 1534, the 'Act of Supremacy' gave the king the title of 'Supreme Head of the Church of England on Earth', and gave the king the power to correct errors in the church and to conduct ecclesiastical visitations. The 'Act of Conditional Restraint of Annates', also passed in 1534, transferred to the king the 'First Fruits and Tenths' that were previously paid to the Pope. In order to facilitate this transfer Commissioners of the Tenth were appointed throughout the country to establish the taxable value of churches and religious houses. The Commissioners conducted their surveys in the spring and summer of 1535 and their reports were collectively known as the *Valor Ecclesiasticus*.

In the same year, Cromwell was authorised to send Visitors to enquire into all the monasteries, abbeys and priories to assess their superstitious observances, such as the ownership of religious relics, and to inquire into their sexual morality.

For the North of England, Cromwell chose as his Visitors Richard Layton, a secular cleric who held clerkships in Chancery and the Privy Council, and Thomas Legh, a lawyer and diplomat, and they proceeded together during Christmas 1535. The Visitors interviewed individually each member of the religious houses, and their servants, with tales to tell or scores to settle, urging them all to confess to all manner of sexual deviancy and to inform on one another. The Visitors were deeply unpopular.

Following their visitations the reports they sent back to Cromwell were collectively known as the *Compendium Compertorum*, and although they took all accusations at face value, no matter how exaggerated, it appears they never fabricated evidence directly.

Parliament met on 4 February 1535/36 and received digests of the *Valor Ecclesiasticus* and the *Compendium Compertorum*, and soon after passed the 'Act for the Dissolution of the Lesser Monasteries', commonly known as the 'Suppression Act', which were defined as those in the *Valor Ecclesiasticus* as having a clear annual income under £200.

All the above stages will now be discussed, as they applied to Thicket Priory.

The return for Thicket in the *Valor Ecclesiasticus* shows that the clear annual value of the priory was the second smallest of the East Riding nunneries, at only £20 8s. 10d. (only Nunburnholme was smaller). The valuation also listed some rents whose origin have yet to be identified, viz.: 6s. in Lepton (Leppington, in the parish of Scrayingham); 2s. 6d. in Cliff; 6s. in Spaldington; 10s. in Allerthorpe; 42s. 4d. in Bennetland; and 10s. in Bellasize (Bellyce).

John Aske was the son and heir of Sir Robert Aske, who died 21 February 1530/31. In the *Inquisition Post Mortem* of Sir Robert, it is stated that he held lands and rents in Goodmanham and West Cottingwith, Bellasize and Benetland, (which descended to him through the marriage of German Haye and Alice de Aske at the end of the fourteenth century). The full entry for Thicket Priory was as follows:

Priory of the Nuns of Thickhead, Katherine, Prioress, County of Yorks

Value	£	s.	d.
Site of the priory with gardens, mills, meadows and glebe annexed, with their own hands occupied in the soil.		100	
Manors, townships, etc			
West Cottingwith	4	15	10
Thorganby		20	
Sutton upon Derwent		14	6
Youlton		6	
Norton		42	
Lepton (Leppington)		6	
Sand Hutton		60	
Greenhammerton		10	
Cliff		2	6
Osgodby		5	
Escrick		36	
Spaldington		6	
Allerthorpe		10	
City of York		6	
Bennetland		42	4
Bellasize		10	
Total	**23**	**12**	**2**
Outgoings	**£**	**s.**	**d.**
Fee of William Percy, chief-lord		20	
Fee of Thomas Doune, receiver		6	8
Fee of John Aske, bailiff		26	8
Total		**53**	**4**
Clear Value	**20**	**8**	**10**

The Outgoings consisted of the rents resolute to the chief lords, which included Sir William Percy, the chief lord, who was the tenant-in-chief of the king, in whose fee Thicket was located; the receiver, Thomas Doune was clerk to Sir William, and was responsible for the collection of all monies; John Aske was the bailiff, who was responsible for ensuring that the lands were managed efficiently. His fee was equal to the two senior positions of chief-lord and receiver combined, suggesting that John Aske was the official who actually did the most work.

It is also noticeable that there is no *Spiritualia* for Thicket. They owned no churches, no advowsons, no tithes, and no other spiritual dues or oblations.

The Visitors entered Yorkshire in early January 1536, and were recorded as being with the Archbishop of York at Cawood 11 January. It was the practice of the Visitors not to visit every religious house at the site of the house, but to send letters in advance requesting the monks and nuns of each house to assemble and meet at some convenient location. Several houses, including Thicket, all within a ten mile radius of York, were examined while the Visitors were at York, and which they completed before 19 January. By the end of February 1536 the Visitation of the Northern Province was over, and Leyton and Legh returned to London. The report from the Visitors for Thicket in the *Compendium Compertorum* was brief:

Matilda Chapman petit dimitti a jugo religionis.
Fundator Johannes Aske
Reddit annuus xxiiil

Matilda Chapman seeks release from the yoke of religion.
Founder John Aske
Annual Rents £23

John Aske was the current patron of Thicket Priory, a title which had descended to him through the former estates of the Haye family, which passed to the Aske family through the childless marriage of German Hay and Alice de Aske at the end of the fourteenth century; and before that had descended from the actual founder, Roger son of Roger, to his sister Emma, who married Roger Hay, as we have seen in the Foundation of Thicket Priory section of this chapter.

Following the *Valor Ecclesiasticus* and the *Compendium Compertorum*, the 'Suppression of Religious Houses Act' or the 'Act for the Dissolution of the Lesser Monasteries', as it was known, was passed by Parliament in February 1535/6. However, Clause XIII of the Act stated the following:

> XIII Provided always, that the king's highness, at any time after the making of this act, may at his pleasure ordain and declare, by his letters patents under his great seal, that such of the said religious houses which his highness shall not be disposed to have suppressed nor dissolved by authority of this act, shall still continue, remain, and be in the same body corporate, and in the said essential estate, quality, and condition, as well in possessions as otherwise, as they were afore the making of this Act...

The Act also provided for the appointment of local commissioners or Particular Receivers to visit the houses under the £200 threshold and report back. The Articles for these commissioners required them to establish their authority over each head of each religious house by exhibiting the Act, and swear them to answer all their questions fully and honestly. The commissioners were to undertake an inventory of all immovable assets (lands and buildings, etc.), and movable assets (plate, jewels, bells, money, furniture, farming stock and other goods). They were then required to question each member of the religious house as to whether they wished to be moved to another house of the same order, or to return to the secular life with a pension. The commissioners then took possession of the seal of the house, together with all plate, jewels and money, to be kept 'in a safe place', and commanded each house to continue tilling and sowing until the king's pleasure be known. No list of the plate, jewels, bells etc. of Thicket is known to exist. It is known that they did have, at least, a communion cup, worth 4½ marks for their chapel, granted by King Henry III in January 1252; and nine-foot torches, left to Thicket in the will of John Croxton of York in March 1393. The commissioners then sent all this information on each house back to London and to await further instructions.

After analysis of these Commissioner's Reports or 'brief certificates' some thirty-three religious houses in Yorkshire were found to be liable to be suppressed, being under the £200 clear annual value threshold, but only fifteen houses of this total of were immediately suppressed. These fifteen had all their movables sold, save the plate, jewels and money, and their heads sent to the alternative houses of their choice, and the rest to the Archbishop of Canterbury or the Lord Chancellor to learn their 'capacities' (rewards for surrendering). That left eighteen to survive. Seven of these eighteen were granted Letters Patent of exemption, in accordance with the above Clause XIII of the Act, and a further three had 'special' status. That left eight houses that had no formal or 'special' exemption. These were Basedale, Esholt, Grosmont, Handale, Thicket, Wilberfoss, Wykeham and Yeddingham.

When all these eight were finally dissolved along with the greater monasteries in 1539 the reason given was to be compliant with the earlier 'Suppression of Religious Houses Act' of 1536. The seven who were granted Letters Patent were treated specifically within the 1539 Act, showing that the eight that had survived up to that Act had no formal status.

The reason why the eight houses, including Thicket, survived the first 1536 Act has been explored by Woodward, who found that the local Particular Receivers mainly responsible for the Yorkshire suppressions, Leonard Beckwith and Hugh Fuller, had a set of instructions which contained the following intriguing sentence, which he believed concerned the above eight houses, 'which our sovereign lord the king hath promised to continue with t... religious persons of them still yet remaining in...without any confirmation or establishment by the King's letters p...thereof made'. This document suggests that the king had made verbal promises to the eight, but for some reason had never issued formal Letters Patent.

When all the remaining Greater and Lesser Monasteries had finally been persuaded (or intimidated) by the commissioners to surrender through 1537–1539, the final 'Act for the Dissolution of Abbeys' was passed in the autumn of 1539, which simply ratified what the Particular Receivers had managed to accomplish. The eight surviving lesser houses in Yorkshire were not mentioned, as they were still under the provisions of the earlier 1536 Act, and their suppression had been simply completed before the 1539 Act.

Thicket Priory was one of the last to be surrendered, being surrendered by the prioress, Agnes Beckwith, on 27 August 1539.

Following the surrender of Thicket Priory the immovable assets were listed and entered in the List of the Lands of Dissolved Religious Houses, which was one category of entries in the List of Ministers' Accounts. The list was made from the earliest account available following the surrender, and in the case of Thicket Priory it was the first account. Rents from the immovable assets were:

> Farm of the site of the priory and demesne lands, with a mill.
>
> Rents and farms in Westcotyngwithe, Benett Lande, Belyces, Alkerthorpe, Thorgunbye, Sutton upon Dervent, Lepyngton, Norton, Sandhutton (including a tenement or manor), Grene Hamerton, in Copergate and without Mikilgate in the City of York, Yotton, Osgodbye, Cliff, Escreyke, Bowton, Draxe by Clyff, Wheldrik and Spawdyngton.

As can be seen, the property owned by the priory generating rental income loosely matches that of the list in the *Valor Ecclesiasticus* above, but gives a little more detail. It specifies the areas where their property lay in the City of York, and additionally gives land holdings in Bowton (possibly Bolton, in the parish of Bishop Wilton, two miles north-west of Pocklington), Drax and Wheldrake.

Only the heads of houses (i.e. abbots, priors or prioresses) were offered pensions in 1536 if they voluntarily surrendered. However, in the case of nunneries it soon became very clear to the commissioners that the nuns had no other religious avenue open to them, other than going to another nunnery, but as no nunnery in the country had a clear annual value of over £200 then dispersal to other houses was simply not possible. Consequently, all later surrenders of nunneries were conditional upon all the nuns receiving a pension, and so it was with Thicket Priory.

Following the dissolution of Thicket in 1539, each of the nuns was granted a 'reward' and a pension. However, as can be seen from the following two lists, the pension of the last prioress, Agnes Beckwith, was the subject of some revision, rising from an initial pension of 53s. 4d. offered by the commissioners in 1536, to an increased pension of 56s. 8d. at the dissolution of Thicket in 1539, then to £6 13s. 4d. when the pension granted was enrolled in the Court of Augmentations. None of the other nuns had their pensions revised in this way.

Could Agnes Beckwith, and the Receiver, Leonard Beckwith, be related? It certainly looks like someone influential was lobbying on behalf of Agnes.

Pensions in 1539

Name	Pension	Reward
Agnes Beckwith, prioress	53s. 4d. (struck out) 56s. 8d. (struck out)	20s.
Alicia Yonge	33s. 4d.	13s. 4d.
Margaret Kychynman	26s. 8d.	10s.
Elena Sterkey	26s. 8d.	10s.
Matilda Chapman	20s.	10s.
Agnes Hunsley	20s.	10s.
Margaret Swale	20s.	10s.
Isabella Cawton	20s.	10s.
Elena Fisher	20s.	10s.

Pensions Enrolled in the Augmentation Books 1539–40

Name	Pension
Agnes Beckwith, prioress	£6 13s. 4d.
Alicia Yonge	33s. 4d.
Margaret Kychynman	26s. 8d.
Elena Sterkey	26s. 8d.
Matilda Chapman	20s.
Agnes Hunsley	20s.
Margaret Swale	20s.
Isabella Cawton	20s.
Elena Fisher	20s.

Most, if not all, simply returned to secular life, with some marrying and some going back to live with their families. We simply do not know, as their names vanish from the public record, except in the records of their pension receipts.

Pension Lists to 1582

Name	Pension	1553 List	1556 List	1564 List	1582 List
Agnes Beckwith	£6 13s. 4d.	✓	✓	✓	
Alice Yong	33s. 4d.				
Margaret Kytchynman	26s. 8d.	✓	✓		
Ellen Starkye	26s. 8d.	✓	✓	✓	✓
Matilda Chapman	20s.	✓	✓	✓	✓
Agnes Hunsley	20s.	✓	✓	✓	
Marjory Swale	20s.	✓	✓	✓	✓
Isabella Cawton	20s.	✓	✓	✓	
Ellen Fyssher	20s.	✓	✓		

Lists of the surviving pensioners of Thicket exist for 1552/3, 1556, 1564 and 1582. Of the nine original pensioners in 1539, eight were still drawing their pension in 1553 and 1556, six in 1564, and just three in 1582: Ellen Starkey; Matilda Chapman; and Marjory Swale, who were now all aged in their seventies.

Thicket Priory had survived for over 350 years, and its last nun would have died over 400 years since its foundation, but she was not to be the last nun to reside at Thicket.

Nuns being evicted following the Dissolution — Alamy

CHAPTER 2

Dissolution to Thicket Priory II

The Aftermath of the Dissolution – The Aske Family – The Robinson Family – The Jefferson Family
The Dunnington Family – Change of Name – Thicket and Ellerton Estate Buildings

The Aftermath of the Dissolution

At the start of Henry's decision to suppress the monasteries, preparations were put in place to handle the huge amount of lands and property that would then come directly to the king and Henry procured two Acts of Parliament. The first Act was to create the Court of Augmentations, and to make it a court of record, and the second Act was for the actual suppression of the lesser monasteries, 'An Acte wherby all Relygeous Houses of Monks Chanons and Nonnes whiche may not dyspend Manors Lande Tents & Heredytaments above the clere yerly Value of ij C li. are geven to the Kings Highnes his heires and Successours for ever', known generally as 'The Suppression of Religious Houses Act, 1535'.

The Court of Augmentations was modelled on that of the Exchequer and its initial purpose was to reward those who had assisted the king's designs and to provide for the subsistence of the abbots, priors and monks, and their female counterparts, who had been turned out of their houses. The scope of the Court was over all the dissolved religious houses and purchased religious houses, with authority to take surrenders of leases and Letters Patent, and grant fresh leases of not more than twenty-one years, with accustomed rents, or to grant at fee-farm or sell at fee simple. Fee-farm grants were effectively a cross between leasehold and freehold; leasehold in that they were subject to rents and covenants, and freehold in that they were without term — they were leases forever, as opposed to fee simple which was freehold, absolute and unqualified. All income raised from the grants of fee-farm was reserved to the king.

But while the tenants of the lands of the religious houses could simply have their leases renewed, at the accustomed rents, the sites of the religious houses themselves now needed new tenants or buyers. The Court of Augmentations moved quickly to take over the existing tenancies in order to provide instant revenue for the crown, followed quickly by sub-leasing to individuals, on favourable terms, so the Court had only one lessee to deal with rather than many smaller tenancies. Sales of monastic lands came later still as the Court's commissioners established their valuation.

A cursory study of these fresh grants of sub-leases in the Letters and Papers of Henry VIII shows that a large proportion of these new sub-leases went to the various clerks of the Chancery, Exchequer and Household, and this was the case concerning Thicket Priory.

William Wytham, a Gentleman Usher of the King's Chamber and bailiff of the borough of Darlington, hailed from Beltonby in the parish of Barton, Richmondshire, six miles S.W. of Darlington. He came from the noted family of Witham of Garforth and Wytham of Lartington Hall, and his great grandfather was Thomas Witham, Chancellor of the Exchequer. Wytham had no traceable connection to Thicket, but the Court of Augmentations granted the lease of the priory to him 20 February 1539/40.

Wytham was to hold his lease until 3 April 1542, when John Aske, the patron of Thicket at the Dissolution, acquired it in fee simple, along with other properties in Yorkshire, in exchange for his manors in Sussex:

Possessions Exchanged

John Aske	Manors of Deane, Verdeley, Sholvestrode, Bestonour, all in the county of Sussex.
The King	The farm of Cleving, late the Preceptory of Beverley, parcel of the Priory of St. John of Jerusalem; site of the Priory of Ellerton and demesnes in the parishes of Ellerton and Aughton, Lathome in Aughton, West Cottingwith, Holme, Goodmanham, Huggate, Thorganby, all late of the Priory of Ellerton; the mansion of Bisshophill in the city of York, parcel of the Priory of Bolton; site and demesnes of the Priory of Thicket; Manor of Dighton, late of St. Mary in the suburbs of York, all in the county of Yorkshire.

A detailed description of the lands that John Aske acquired from the king in this exchange exists, in the records of the Court of Augmentations, and the entry for the trees about *The Scyte and demesnes of the late priory of Thyckhed in the seid countie* (of Yorks) were described as follows:

> *The trees growing aboute the scytuacion of the seid late pryorye and fences and in hedges inclosyng landes perteynyng to the same wyll barely suffyce for tymber to repayre the houses standyng uppon the scyte of the seid late pryorye and fences and to mayntane the hedges and fences aboute the same therfore not val.*

The full Patent Roll entry for this exchange also gives more detail for the Thicket Priory part of the exchange, and includes the information that the site and demesnes of Thicket included a windmill, and named closes lying or being in Thickhede [Thicket] and West Cottingwith, noting that all land acreages are estimates:

One close of land & pasture called the Myln Flatt of 10 acres

One close of land & pasture called le Acorne close of 4 acres

One other close of land & pasture of 14 acres between the Myln Flatt and le Acorne close

8 acres of arable land & pasture on Le Fountaine dykes in divers places

Two parcels of land called Skowe Flatts of 4½ acres

Two parcels of parkland lying in the fields there of 4 acres

One close of land & pasture called Le Gyngle close of 12 acres

3 parcels of land on le More Butts in Astylfel called Westowe of 3 acres

One close of land and pasture called Lyttleinge croft of 3 acres

One other close of land and pasture called Allergddynge otherwise called le Whynney close of 14 acres

One other close of land and pasture called le Wheate close otherwise called Fogge close, of 8 acres

One other close of land and pasture called le Cowe close of 10 acres

One other close of land and pasture called le Kylne Garth of 2 acres

One other close of land and pasture called Le Haverclose otherwise called the le Coney close of 12 acres

One other close of land and pasture called Sycome of 8 acres

One other close of meadow and pasture called le Crofte of 10 acres

One other close of land and pasture called le Tongue of 10 acres

One other close of land and pasture called Calfe Close of 1 acre

4 acres of meadow & pasture in le Lytle Mershe

5 acres of meadow & pasture in a certain place called divers hills

6 acres of meadow and pasture in Cottingwith Ings

7 acres of meadow and pasture in Wheldrake banks.

The Aske Family

The patrons of Thicket Priory and the nearby Gilbertine priory of Ellerton were intricately linked through the Hay and Aske families. To recap from Chapter 1, Thicket was founded by Roger, son of Roger son of Alured in the late twelfth century. The founder's brother and sister, Thomas and Emma, were also major benefactors. With the death of the founder without issue, and the death of Thomas, son of Thomas, also without issue, the patronage fell to the sole surviving benefactor, Emma, who married Roger Hay, and the patronage then continued through their son, Thomas Hay, then his son, another Roger Hay (died 1247x1251).

Shortly after the foundation of Thicket Priory, Ellerton Priory, on the other side of the Derwent River, was founded by William son of Peter. William died without issue and so the patronage of Ellerton came to William's sister, Agnes, who married Adam de Linton (died 1225x1231). Their daughter, Christiana de Linton, married the last named Roger Hay above (died 1247x1251). This marriage of Christiana de Linton and Roger Hay united the patronages of Thicket Priory and Ellerton Priory in one family — the Hay family. The tree showing the connections between the above families has been published by Carpenter.

The patronage of Thicket and Ellerton continued in the Hay family until German Hay of Aughton married Alice Aske, daughter of John Aske of Owsthorpe.

The Aske family then became possessed of Aughton through the marriage settlement of German Hay and Alice Aske, dated 1 October 1386 (10 Ric. II), which stated that, in the event of there being no issue to this marriage, the reversion of Aughton should go to John de Aske, father of the said Alicia and his heirs. German Hay and Alicia had no issue, and the manor and patronages came to the Aske family of Aughton. The manor of Aughton then descended from John Aske, the father of Alicia through his son John Aske who married Elizabeth Gascoigne, and their son Richard, who married Margaret Ughtred, and their son Sir John Aske, who married Elizabeth Bigod, and their son Sir Robert Aske, who married Elizabeth, daughter of John, Lord Clifford.

Descendancy Tree for Sir Robert Aske of Aughton (d. 1530/1)

1. Sir Robert Aske of Aughton, Yorks. m. c. 1481, Elizabeth, dau. of John, Lord Clifford, 9th Baron Clifford. Sir Robert made his will 16 Mar 1529 and died 21 Feb 1530/1, probate granted 16 Mar 1541. Requested to be buried in the quire of Aughton church next to his wife. Children: 4 sons — John, Christopher, Robert, Richard; 7 daughters — Margaret, Anne, Agnes, Dorothy, Mary, Eleanor and Elizabeth.

    1.1 John Aske of Aughton Esq. with lands in Sussex. m. before 1520, Eleanor Ryther, dau. of Sir Ralph Ryther. Exchanged his Sussex lands with Henry VIII, for various lands, including the sites of Ellerton Priory and Thicket Priory. Made his will, dated 20 Nov 1543, died 5 Mar 1543/4, probate 28 Mar 1544. Children: 5 sons and 3 daughters.

    1.2 Christopher Aske of Loundesburge Esq. Unmarried. Made his will 19 Jul 1538, probate 26 Jun 1540.

    1.3 Richard Aske alive in 1507 but died young.

    1.4 Robert Aske of Aughton. Unmarried. Trained as a lawyer, admitted Gray's Inn 1527. Leader of the Pilgrimage of Grace. No will. Executed, hung in chains on a special gibbet outside Clifford's Tower, York, 12 Jul 1537.

It was with Sir Robert's children that the site of Thicket Priory came into the Aske family following the Dissolution. Of the four sons of Sir Robert, Richard died young, leaving three who grew to adulthood. John Aske, the elder of the three surviving brothers, and heir to Sir Robert, held an ambiguous position during the upheavals of the Reformation. The middle son Christopher was for the king, while the youngest, Robert, went on to become the leader of the main resistance to the Reformation, heading the uprising known as the Pilgrimage of Grace.

The three brothers were quite close prior to the Reformation, enjoying a comfortable life, and often went hunting together with their brother-in-law, William Ellerker, and their cousin, Sir Ralph Ellerker the younger. It was following one such hunting party in the East Riding on 3 October 1536 that Robert Aske was intercepted by the Pilgrims on his way back to his legal practice in London, and forced to sign their oath, declaring him to be their 'captain'. Unlike others that reneged on the oath, being forced to sign under duress, Robert Aske actually became convinced of the religious convictions of the Pilgrims and took up their cause wholeheartedly.

However, Robert's brother, Christopher Aske, was servant to his cousin, Henry Clifford, the 1st Earl of Cumberland, and was one of the earl's receivers, possibly his steward. Mervyn James described Christopher as the earl's 'man of business' and also kept his courts.

The earl was for the king and his seat at Skipton Castle was the only great castle in the northern parts that remained faithful to the king during the Pilgrimage of Grace. Christopher Aske was the earl's loyal servant, and of this there can be no doubt. One particular event serves to illustrate his loyalty: the earl had, perhaps naively, sent his daughter-in-law, the Lady Eleanor (the king's niece) and her young son, two of the earl's daughters and other gentlewomen, to Bolton Abbey, close to the earl's other main residence at Barden Tower, thinking they would be safer there.

However, the Pilgrims somehow heard of this, and finding Skipton impregnable planned to capture and bring the earl's family before the walls of Skipton Castle, hoping to lure out the defenders, and if that failed, 'to violate and enforce them with knaves, unto my Lords great discomfort.' However, Christopher, along with the vicar of Skipton, a groom and a boy, found a way through the enemy lines, and rescued the unfortunate women and children from Bolton Abbey, bringing them by unfrequented paths back to the castle.

The Pilgrimage of Grace – The Pilgrims enter London

Descendancy Tree for John Clifford, 9th Baron Clifford

1. John Clifford, 9th Baron Clifford, 9th Lord of Skipton. m. Margaret Blomeflete. John Clifford died 28 March 1461. Children: 2 sons — Henry, Richard; 1 daughter — Elizabeth.

    1.1 Henry Clifford, 10th Baron Clifford. m. 1st Anne St. John — she died in 1508. 2nd Florence Pudsey. Henry Clifford died 23 April 1523. Children: (By Anne) 2 sons — Henry, Thomas, 4 daughters; (By Florence) 1 daughter.

    1.1.1 Henry Clifford, 11th Baron Clifford, later 1st Earl of Cumberland. m. 1st Margaret Talbot, daughter of the 4th Earl of Shrewsbury. Margaret died before 1516; m. 2nd Margaret Percy, daughter of Henry Percy, 5th Earl of Northumberland. Henry Clifford died 1542. Children: (By Margaret Talbot) nil; (By Margaret Percy) 7, including Henry.

    1.1.1.1 Henry Clifford, 2nd Earl of Cumberland. m. 1st Lady Eleanor Brandon, second daughter of Charles Brandon, 1st Duke of Suffolk, by his third wife, Mary Tudor, former Queen Consort of France. Lady Eleanor died 27 September 1547. m. 2nd Anne Dacre, daughter of William Dacre, 3rd Baron Dacre. Henry Clifford died shortly after 8 January 1569/70. Children: (By Lady Eleanor) 2 sons, both dying in infancy; 1 daughter — Lady Margaret Clifford; (By Anne Dacre) 2 sons — George Clifford, 3rd Earl of Cumberland, Francis Clifford, 4th Earl of Cumberland; 1 daughter — Lady Frances Clifford.

    1.2 Elizabeth Clifford, m. c. 1481 Sir Robert Aske of Aughton.

The ultimate failure of the rebellion known as the Pilgrimage of Grace, the retribution of Henry VIII, and the hanging in chains of the leader of the rebellion, Robert Aske, at Clifford's Tower in York in July 1537, have all been well documented and well authored, but not so well on the two surviving brothers, John and Christopher.

Little is known about Christopher Aske following the Pilgrimage of Grace. We know that he rebuilt Aughton church tower after the rebellion, upon which is a somewhat ambiguous inscription in Old French:

Cristofer le second fitz de Robert Ask chr oblier ne doy Ao. Di. 1536.

The inscription has two possible translations, of which I am inclined towards the first:

(1) 'I (the tower) ought not to forget Christofer, second son of Robert Aske, chevalier, A.D. 1536'
(2) 'Christofer, the second son of Robert Aske, chevalier, I ought not to forget, A.D. 1536'

Christopher Aske made his will 19 July 1538, and died shortly before 27 Feb 1539/40, with probate being granted the following 26 June 1540. He left his manor in Loundesborough to his brother John Aske, and several other bequests to other beneficiaries, including Lord Henry Clifford. Several of his bequests were of goods in his chambers at Skipton Castle and Bolton.

Following the death of Christopher, John Aske was the sole surviving heir of their father, Sir Robert Aske, who had died 21 February 1530/1. John Aske was indifferent to the Reformation, being only concerned with his family and his lands, but he was firmly against the rebellion as this threatened both. Robert's insurrection did not affect him; on the contrary he took advantage of the fall of the monasteries to consolidate his Yorkshire estates, and in 1541 exchanged his manors in Sussex for the sites of the priories of Ellerton and Thicket and other church lands in Yorkshire, as we have seen in the previous chapter.

John Aske made his last will 20 November 1543 and died 5 March 1543/4. Probate of his will was granted the following 18 March 1543/4. John Aske had a large family, five sons and three daughters: Robert Aske of Aughton; Richard Aske of Ousethorpe; Christopher; Anthony; John; Anne; Elizabeth and Julian, the wife of Thomas Portington. The eldest and heir, Robert Aske, predeceased his father, dying in 1542 (Robert Aske's will is dated 20 Sep 1542, and probate was granted 2 Oct 1542), so the bulk of the lands of John Aske descended to his grandson, Robert Aske, the son of the above Robert Aske by his wife, Eleanor, daughter of Sir Ninian Markenfield.

Robert Aske, the grandson of John Aske, went on to become High Sheriff of York in 1588. He married twice, 1st to Elizabeth, the daughter of Sir John Dawney and had by her a son and heir John Aske and two daughters; 2nd to Ellen, daughter of Francis Meering, which produced a further four children. Robert was a co-heir of his great-uncle Henry Ryther of Ryther, and inherited the manors of Ryther, Ossendike and Stockbridge, plus various other holdings, in 1544. Robert Aske died 31 August 1590, leaving a will.

John Aske, son and heir of Robert Aske, married Christian or Christiana, daughter of Sir Thomas Fairfax of Denton, shortly before 1 March 1581/2 as on that date Robert Aske, by his charter, granted tenements in Ryther, the manor of Deighton, all his lands in Deighton, West Cottingwith, Thorganby, Bubwith and South Duffield, together with the site of Thickhead, to the use of John Aske, his son and heir apparent, and of Christiana daughter of Thomas Fairfax, knight, and wife of the said John. John and Christiana then granted several leases: to William Kirkby of Deighton, 6 June 1585; to Jane Roclif, January 1588/9; and to William Foxgaile, November 1591. However, following that last date they never appear in land transactions again as a couple.

John's father, Robert Aske, died 21 August 1590. In his *Inquisition Post Mortem*, his landholdings were stated to be:
> Manor of Aughton, 20 messuages, 1,000 acres of land, worth £30.
> Manor of Everthorpe, 20 messuages, worth £12.
> Land and tenements in Hithe and Dike, worth 36s. 4d.
> Annual rent from lands in South Duffield, 14s.
> Site of the late priory of Ellerton and 200 acres of land, worth £6 13s. 4d.
> Pasture of sheep called Sheepgates in Killingoth, worth 6s. 8d.
> Manors of Ryther, Ossendike and Stockbridge, worth £50.
> Manor of Deighton, dwellings and 200 acres of land, worth 70s.
> Messauge called Rytherhill, worth £20.
> Capital messuage called Cottingwith Grange, with land, worth £7 14d.
> Tenement and land in Thorganby, worth 29s.
> Four messuages and land in Bubwith and Breighton, worth 43s. 10d.
> Site of the priory of Thickhead, windmill and 150 acres, worth 100s.
> Two tenements and 200 acres of land in Holme, worth 100s.
> Capital messuage, cottage, 200 acres of land, water mill, £8 3s.
> Grange or capital messuage, dwellings and land in Laytham, £6 10s. 8d.
> Toft, croft and 4 bovates of land called Clevinge, worth £8.
> In possession £58 9s. 3d.; tenanted £134 11s. 8d.
> Total: £175 8s.
> In reversion £116 18s. 8d.

John Aske was named as Robert's heir, aged 25 and upwards at the time of the Inquisition, taken at Selby, dated 8 July 1590. John asked for special livery on 1 September which was granted Michaelmas, 1591.

In 1592, John Aske, without his wife, raised money by mortgaging the Manor of Owsthorpe and other lands to Christopher Sowden; this was quickly followed by another mortgage on the Manor of Ellerton with lands in Thicket, to Sir George Saintpoole and Martin Brighouse. Another mortgage was raised in May 1594, to Marmaduke Grymstone, Esq. on Aske's properties in Goodmanham.

John Aske clearly had problems both with his money and with his marriage.

In February 1594 a somewhat unhappy cause was brought before the Ecclesiastical Court of York, by John Aske of Aughton for an annulment of his marriage to Christiana Aske of Weston (they were clearly living apart at this point) on the grounds of Christiana's adultery. John produced several witnesses to support his cause, including a servant from John's estate at Ryther and another from his manor house in Aughton. No result of this matrimonial cause has been found.

Following this attempt at an annulment Aske needed to raise yet more money and mortgaged his manors of Ryther, Ossendike, Stockbridgefeild, and Aughton, together with many dwellings and lands there, to his relatives, Francis Clifford, John Dawney and others. However, from 1596 Aske began to divest himself of almost all his property in Yorkshire. First to go in November 1596 was his manor of Dighton together with the sites of the priories of Ellerton and Thicket, and 50 messuages with lands in Deighton, Ellerton, Aughton, East Cottingwith, West Cottingwith, Thorganby, Wheldrake, and Thykhed, and the free fishing in the Derwent, which he sold to John Robinson senior; and in November 1598 Aske sold his manors of Ryther, Ossendike, Stockbridgefield, and many houses and land, with free fishing in the river Wharfe, and the advowson of Ryther church, to John Robinson junior and Henry Robinson, the sons of John Robinson senior.

Clearly, John Aske was facing mounting problems financially, but 1598 was to prove a watershed year for him legally too, when he faced an accusation of fraud in a case that was brought by John Robinson senior before the Court of Star Chamber. Robinson complained that in September 1596 he entered into discussions with John Aske of Ryther, concerning the purchase of the manor of Deighton, and the sites of Ellerton and Thicket priories along with other lands and premises, for £2,550. Although Robinson did not know Aske personally, he was encouraged to accept this deal by one John Redman of Water Fulford who drove the bargain, and who affirmed that Aske had lands £600 over the asking price, so he (Robinson) accepted the deal and paid the sum requested by an indenture of bargain and sale, with covenants inserted for further assurance. The indenture was drawn up by the advice of Christopher Aske, and sealed and delivered in the presence of the said Christopher Aske and one Thomas Badger. Robinson then went on to say that such a sale should have then resulted in statute staple recognizances being entered into by Aske, to perform the covenants in the indenture, but John Edman, Christopher Aske and Thomas Badger pressured him (Robinson) into forbearing the acknowledgement for some time because Aske was then in some trouble with the Lord Chief Justice of England and the Lord Chief Justice of the Court of Common Pleas, and 'durst not go before either of them, but would shortly after acknowledge the recognizances'. Robinson, doubting nothing, consented to these terms, but before Aske made any acknowledgement, and with the confederacy of John Redman, Christopher Aske, Thomas Badger and one Richard Brackinburie, Aske conveyed all the residue of his lands to Christopher Aske and others, with the intent to defraud the petitioner (Robinson). Aske then entered into recognizances, duly acknowledged by Aske, with Richard Brackinburie, John Redman, and one Raphe Babthorpe. Robinson asked the Court to subpena John Aske, John Redman, Christopher Aske, Richard Brakenburie, and Thomas Badger, to appear and answer.

It is not known how the case unfolded, but eventually Robinson apparently won his case, as later he was in possession of the manor of Deighton and the sites of Ellerton and Thicket priories and the other lands and premises mentioned in the suit.

Sometime after 1601 Aske moved to London, and lived together with one Margaret, daughter of Sir John Gwylliams of Munsterwood in the county of Gloucester. It is probable that John and Margaret had lived together as man and wife before this year, as when he made his will in December 1605 he referred to his 'wife', Margaret Aske als Gwylliams, writing 'who hath these many years demeaned herself to me as a kind and loving wife'. They had a child together, Margaret Aske, and at the time of writing his will his wife Margaret was with child once again. Although living together, and referring to Margaret as his 'wife', they had never married, as he was still legally married to Christian Aske, but no bigamy had occurred. However, the legality of the will was challenged by his legal wife, Christian Aske, in the Prerogative Court of

Canterbury, but the validity of the will was upheld by the Prerogative Court and administration of the will was granted to Margaret.

John Aske died in December 1605, having made his will 16 December 1605, with probate of the will being granted 31 December 1605. The sentence of the Prerogative Court regarding the will was dated 12 February 1606/7.

Past authors simply state that John Aske ran up enormous debts, and sold off all the family's lands, but do not answer the questions of who these debts were to…so was John Aske really a fraudster?

The Robinson Family

This branch of the Robinson family was not native to Yorkshire. They were originally from Staffordshire and eventually settled in London.

John Robinson

John Robinson was a highly successful businessman in London. He was an Alderman, Merchant Taylor, Merchant of the Staple, and as we have seen previously purchased extensive lands in Yorkshire from John Aske in 1596.

John Robinson made his will 12 July 1599, and despite beginning the will with 'in perfect health' he died the following 19 February 1599/1600, aged 70, having been married to his wife, Christian, for 36 years, producing no less than nine sons and seven daughters. There is a monument to him and his wife in St. Helen's Church, Bishopsgate, London, which is still there. However, John's will was challenged by his estranged daughter, Elizabeth, who had 'willfully' married a Mr. Jeffries without her father's consent, and against her father's wishes. She was cut off from the bulk of his estate, and left just £10. Elizabeth was joined in this action by John Robinson junior, the eldest son of John Robinson senior. Elizabeth later dropped out of this suit, but John Robinson junior continued it. However, the validity of the will was upheld by the Prerogative Court of Canterbury, and John Robinson junior was condemned in costs.

In the will of John Robinson senior, dated 12 July 1599, he mentions that he had previously sold 'the lordship of Dighton, the monasterie of Ellerton, the priorie of Thickhed and Cottingwith Graunge, with other landes in Cottingwithe and Thurgamby' to his sons Henry and Arthur. However, these properties were not sold jointly and severally. Arthur was sold the manor of Deighton, and Henry the remainder. The eldest son, John Robinson junior, had bought the manors of Ryther, Ossendyke and Stockbridgefields, directly from John Aske, but John Robinson senior made clear in his will that all the manors his sons had acquired, by purchase or sold to them by their father, were all still not held harmless by John Aske.

Descendancy Tree for John Robinson

1. John Robinson, alderman and Merchant Taylor of London, died 1598.
    - 1.1 John Robinson of Ryther.
    - 1.2 Henry Robinson of London, m. Margaret Coulthurst. Sold the site of Ellerton Priory to Sir Robert Ducie in 1621/2, and the site of Thicket Priory to his brother, Humphrey Robinson, in 1622.
    - 1.3 Arthur Robinson, bought the manor of Deighton from his father before 12 July 1599.
    - 1.4 Robert Robinson, citizen of London and Merchant of the Staple.
    - 1.5 Humphrey Robinson I, died Sept. 1626, m1 (4 Aug 1601, Widford, Herts): Sara Barnes, daughter of Bartholomew Barnes, citizen and mercer of London. Sara died and was buried 20 Jun 1605, St. Bartholomew by the Exchange, London. Two children, one died young the other in infancy.
        - 1.5.1 Bartholomew Robinson, c: 19 Jun 1603; b: 19 Oct 1614, St. Botolph, Bishopsgate, London.
        - 1.5.2 John Robinson, c: 16 Dec 1604; b: 2 Mar 1605/6, St. Bartholomew by the Exchange, London.

        m:2 (12 Nov 1605, St. Bartholomew by the Exchange): Anne Pyott, daughter of Richard Pyott, citzen and alderman of London.

- 1.5.3 Humphrey Robinson, c: 20 Jan 1619, St. Dunstan, Stepney. d.s.p.
- 1.5.4 Richard Robinson senior of Thicket, J.P., aged 52, 9 Sept 1665.
- 1.5.5 Elizabeth Robinson, m:1 William Breary, m:2 Peter Bradley.
- 1.5.6 Anne Robinson.

1.6 Daughters: Katherine, Elizabeth, Christian, Agnes, Marie.

Humphrey Robinson I

By 1619 Humphrey Robinson was residing in 'Bednall Green' [Bethnal Green] and gave this as his place of residence when having his son Humphrey baptised at St. Dunstan and All Saints, Stepney, 20 January 1619. We can be sure this is the correct Humphrey Robinson as a deed exists between Humphrey Robinson of London, merchant, and William Pyott of London concerning the Corner House, in Bednall Green, the capital messuage of the Pyott Estate, which Humphrey was releasing back to the Pyott Estate.

Henry Robinson resided in London and it was probably in order to concentrate his assets there that he sold the site of the late priory of Ellerton, with lands in Ellerton, Aughton, East Cottingwith, West Cottingwith and Thorganby to Sir Robert Ducie during the Hilary Term of 1621/2; and the site of the priory of Thickhead with dwellings and land in Thickhead, West Cottingwith, Thorganby and Wheldrake, to his brother Humphrey Robinson I, during the Michaelmas Term of 1622. Humphrey Robinson and Sir Robert Ducy (Ducie) were brothers-in-law, both having married sisters, Anne Pyott and Elizabeth Pyott, respectively, daughters of Richard Pyott, citizen and alderman of London. They all figure in the will of Richard Pyott, proved 31 Jan 1619/20, in the Prerogative Court of Canterbury.

The sale from Henry Robinson to his brother Humphrey in 1622 did not mention any capital messuage, only 'the site of the late Priory of Thickhead and 8 messuages and 8 cottages'. In addition, the wording of the sale from Henry Robinson to Sir Robert and Humphrey was unclear which led to Sir Robert instituting a suit in Chancery.

Following a survey of the properties an agreement was reached between the parties in May 1623. The agreement was endorsed by 'R R' that he has since purchased the lands in West Cottingwith and Thorganby from Sir William Ducie, the alderman's son. The endorsement referred to the purchase of the Ducie dwellings and lands in West Cottingwith and Thorganby by Richard Robinson, Humphrey's son, in June–August 1659, thus reuniting the Thicket Priory Estate in Wheldrake, West Cottingwith and Thorganby once again.

Humphrey Robinson made his will 5 October 1626 and died two days later, being buried at Wheldrake. His will was probated 3 March 1626/7. There was no mention in the will of a capital messuage, but he did state that he was 'of Thickhead'. When his widow Anne (née Pyott) died in 1636, the burial register of Wheldrake also recorded her as being 'of Thickhead'.

Richard Robinson senior and junior

During the English Civil War and *Interregnum* Richard Robinson took the side of the Parliamentarians. He was a Justice of the Peace between 1647 and 1651, a Chief Justice of the Peace for the East Riding of Yorkshire in the late 1650s, and was returned as one of the four Members of Parliament for the East Riding under Oliver Cromwell's First Protectorate Parliament which began at Westminster on 3 September 1654.

Following the passing of 'An Act touching Marriages and the Registring thereof' in August 1653, all marriages had to performed before a Justice of the Peace, and all births and burials had to be entered into a new register, to replace the traditional parish registers, and kept by a new official, confusingly called the 'Register', described as 'some able and honest person'. In Wheldrake, it was agreed by the parishioners that Richard Robinson, who was already a Justice of the Peace, should also officiate as the Register, and the register of births, burials and marriages from 1654 carries his name on the front cover. Richard also officiated for marriages at other nearby parishes, and it would also appear that marriages were performed at Thicket itself, as the marriage of Arthur Squire and Elizabeth Oglethorpe, 22 February 1654/5, is said by Thomas Burton to have taken place at Thicket.

Richard was also elected as one of the four Members of Parliament for the East Riding, for the First Protectorate Parliament, 1654-5. Richard had also been mooted for the post of High Sheriff of Yorkshire in 1655, but a Colonel Robert Lilburne wrote to Oliver Cromwell informing him that Richard Robinson was 'as one somewhat of a lose conversation, and one that is too much addicted to tippling, and that which is called good-fellowship, and was lately accus'd before the commissioners to be somewhat concerned in point of delinquency.' It would seem these comments had the intended effect, as Richard was passed over for the post of High Sheriff and was dropped as Member of Parliament for the East Riding for the Second Protectorate Parliament, 1656-8.

Before 1656 a capital messuage was built at Thicket, which Richard Robinson brought to the marriage settlement of his younger son, Richard Robinson junior, on his forthcoming marriage to Jane, daughter of John Ayckroyd of Foggathorpe, in November 1656. This was a very substantial house, recorded as having 10 hearths in the Hearth Tax returns of Lady Day 1672.

It was while Richard Robinson senior was in possession of the Thicket Priory Estate that Richard was to present himself to the famous antiquary and herald, Sir William Dugdale, in the September of 1665, in York. Dugdale, as Norroy King of Arms, was conducting his heraldic Visitation of Yorkshire and had summoned the nobility and gentleman of the area to prove their right to bear their heraldic arms. Unfortunately, Richard could not attend due to illness, and wrote to Dugdale twice at York providing evidence of his descent, and it was from information provided by Robinson that Dugdale constructed his Pedigree of the Robinson family. Robinson also included copies of many of the original charters and grants to Thicket, which Dugdale later used in his joint work with Roger Dodsworth, the *Monasticon Anglicanum*.

Arms of Robinson of London and co. York 1634

Descendancy Tree for Richard Robinson senior

1. Richard Robinson senior, c. 1613–1678, J.P., m. Elizabeth, dau of John Bradley of Louth, co. Lincs.
    - 1.1 Richard Robinson junior, c. 18 Apr 1639, Wheldrake, b. 17 Aug 1679, m. Jane, dau of John Ackroyd of Foggathorpe.
        - 1.1.1 Humphrey Robinson, aged 3 months on 9 Sep 1665, b. Wheldrake, 20 Apr 1705, m. Rebecca, dau of Nicholas Moore (More).
            - 1.1.1.1 Humphrey.
            - 1.1.1.2 Richard.
            - 1.1.1.3 Henry.
            - 1.1.1.4 Nicholas, c. 9 Jun 1704, at Wheldrake.
            - 1.1.1.5 Mary Robinson, m. Hugh Palliser of North Deighton.
        - 1.1.2 Elizabeth Robinson, m. Timothy Johnson, rector of Bubwith.
    - 1.2 Jane Robinson, m. Henry Edmunds of Worsbrough.

In 1672 Richard senior placed Cottingwith Grange, along with 3 cottages and land in West Cottingwith and a messuage in Thorganby, in trust, for his own use for life, then to his wife Elizabeth for life in lieu of dower, and then to son and heir Richard Robinson junior, for life, with remainder to Humphrey Robinson son and heir of Richard Robinson junior. 1672 was also the year that Richard Robinson senior was assessed for the Hearth Tax, levied on Lady Day of that year, when his mansion in West Cottingwith was returned as containing 10 hearths. This was almost certainly Thicket Priory II, later to be known as Thicket Hall, and no other capital messuages were listed in West Cottingwith. Richard Robinson, Esq., senior, died and was buried at Wheldrake, 24 November 1678, and his son, Richard Robinson, Esq., junior, was also buried there less than a year later, 17 Aug 1679. Unfortunately, neither left a will, but a grant was made to Jane Robinson, the widow of Richard Robinson junior, for the administration of his goods and chattels. She was also given tuition or curation of their younger children Alice, Susanna, Mary and Richard, 5 November 1679.

Humphrey Robinson II

Richard Robinson junior's son and heir, Humphrey Robinson II, became active in the real estate of the area from 1680 onwards, and regularly from 1687. In 1690 Humphrey married Rebecca Moore of York, a spinster, and their marriage settlement included a mansion house in Thickhead with messuages, closes and lands in West Cottingwith, Thorganby, Thickhead and Foggerthorpe, for her marriage portion of £1,500. They married by licence 15 September 1690 at Monk Frystone. Humphrey posted a bond for £3,000 to perform his covenants under the marriage settlement, which was normally set at double the value of the the assets he brought, i.e. £1,500, matching that of his bride to be, which indicates the value of the mansion and much of the Thicket Priory Estate at that time.

Humphrey immediately used Rebecca's large dowry to good effect. Some he loaned out with good returns and some he used to buy more houses and land in West Cottingwith, all through his attorneys in York, Nicholas Suger and Thomas Bradley, whom he had been using before his marriage.

It was around the turn of the century that we first learn of dealings between Humphrey Robinson and Thomas Dunnington senior and junior, and in 1716 the first dealings between Humphrey Robinson junior and Thomas Dunnington.

In July 1721 Humphrey Robinson senior created a trust for his younger children, Henry, Nicholas and Rebecca. The property in the trust consisted of a capital messuage, two barns, kiln, dovecot and named closes in Thickett, 12 beastgates on West Cottingworth Common, and 7 acres called Nun Ings in Wheldrake Ings. This trust was designed to secure payments of the children's portions. A similar trust was set up in May 1725 to cater for Richard Robinson, the next eldest son (and heir of his elder brother, Humphrey), and elder daughters, Mary, who was married to Hugh Palliser of North Deighton, and Rebecca, who between the first trust and this had married Jacob Custobodie of York. The property in the trust was exactly the same as in the earlier trust.

It is interesting that Richard Robinson, the second eldest son of Humphrey senior, is described as heir of his elder brother Humphrey junior, suggesting that Humphrey junior was unmarried, or without any children. Humphrey Robinson died and was buried 11 May 1723 at Wheldrake.

Nicholas Robinson, his highs and lows

Humphrey Robinson's third son, Nicholas Robinson, was baptised 9 June 1704 at Wheldrake, and as a young man of 23 he joined the Royal Navy passing his lieutenant's examination in 1725, taking his first post as third lieutenant of HMS *Nottingham* 16 February 1726/7. His naval career was intermittently interrupted when he was elected M.P. for Wootton Bassett from April 1734–May 1741, while still serving as a naval officer. He was promoted to captain and commanding officer of the frigate HBMS *Aldborough* in May 1735 before becoming the captain and commanding officer of the 20-gun HBMS *Kennington* in June, 1737. He was appointed as deputy lord lieutenant of the East Riding of Yorkshire 6 August 1739, again while still serving as a naval officer. In December 1740 he was promoted yet again, becoming briefly the captain and commanding officer of the 50-gun ship of the line HBMS *Tiger*, before taking command of the even larger 70-gun ship of the line HBMS *Essex* the following February.

While a serving as lieutenant on the *Nottingham* he married Sarah Collingwood, the widow of William Collingwood, Esq., and daughter of William Vavasour of Weston. They married by licence at St. Mary Bishophill Senior, York, in February 1728. Sarah died childless and intestate and the administration of her effects was granted 27 Jun 1730 to her husband, Nicholas. Some time later, Nicholas began an affair with his housekeeper, a Mrs. Sarah Brearer, and in 1735 she gave birth to a daughter, another Sarah, of whom more later.

The career of Nicholas in the Royal Navy came to abrupt end in June 1743, when he was court-martialled at Sheerness and fined 12 months' pay for defrauding the Government of £138 18s. by false accounts.

Hugh Palliser, son of Hugh Palliser and Mary née Robinson

Hugh Palliser was born at Kirk Deighton, 22 February 1722/3, the son of Hugh Palliser and Mary, née Robinson, the sister of Nicholas Robinson. His parents died while Hugh was an infant, the father dying a few months after his son's birth in 1723, and his mother two years later in 1725, leaving Hugh and his four sisters as orphans. The orphans were almost certainly raised by their maternal relatives, the Robinsons of Thicket Priory. In May 1725 a trust was set up for Hugh for £800, charged upon the Thicket Priory Estate.

Hugh joined the Royal Navy in 1735 as a midshipman on the *Aldborough*, commanded by his uncle Nicholas, and followed his uncle to the *Kennington* in 1737, and then to the *Tiger* and *Essex*. Palliser passed his lieutenant's examination 12 May 1741 and was promoted to that rank on 18 September 1741 and continued to serve aboard the *Essex*.

Senior positions followed rapidly, including captain of HMS *Weazel*, February 1746; post-captain of HMS *Captain*, November 1746; captain of the 50-gun HMS *Bristol* in early 1752; the command of the 58-gun HMS *Eagle*, October 1755; and the command of the 74-gun HMS *Shrewsbury*, part of the Channel Fleet, in March 1758.

In 1764 Palliser was made Commodore Governor and Commander-in-Chief of Newfoundland, which included command of the 50-gun HMS *Guernsey*, and several frigates.

Palliser remained Governor of Newfoundland until 1768. On 6 August 1770 Commodore Palliser was appointed Comptroller of the Navy, and on 25 June 1773 was elevated to the dignity of baronet. Palliser was a staunch supporter of the Whigs, and was elected to Parliament for the Borough of Scarborough in 1774. On 31 March 1775 he achieved flag rank when promoted to rear-admiral, and joined the Board of Admiralty as First Naval Lord in April 1775, receiving the sinecure office of Lieutenant-General of Marines. Palliser was promoted to vice-admiral on 29 January 1778.

In 1778 Palliser was appointed to the Channel Fleet under Admiral Augustus Keppel. On 27 July 1778 in the First Battle of Ushant, the Channel Fleet fought an inconclusive battle with the French fleet. The battle's outcome led to personal acrimony between Palliser and Keppel who were formerly good friends. The dispute resulted in their individual courts martial and Palliser was forced to resign from Parliament and his other posts. Palliser was eventually acquitted and hoped to be reinstated as Lieutenant-General of Marines. Instead, in 1780 he was appointed Governor of Greenwich Hospital and was again elected to Parliament, this time for Huntingdon, holding the post until 1784. On 24 September 1787 he was promoted to full admiral.

Association with James Cook

James Cook, a fellow Yorkshireman, first served under Palliser as Master's Mate of HMS *Eagle* from 1755 to 1758. Palliser would have supported his elevation to Master in 1757. Both were present at the Siege of Quebec where Cook charted the approach to the city and the landing area. Following the Treaty of Paris, Cook was charged with surveying Newfoundland. As Governor, Palliser actively supported Cook's work and assisted in the publication of his acclaimed map of Newfoundland. During his term as Comptroller, Palliser supported Cook's first command of exploration in 1768, and his subsequent voyages. Cook named Cape Palliser, Palliser Bay and Palliser Isles after his 'worthy friend'. On Cook's death, Palliser erected a memorial to Cook at the Vache, his estate near Chalfont St. Giles in Buckinghamshire.

Palliser died on 19 March 1796 on his Vache estate and was buried on 26 March 1796 at the parish church of St. Giles where there is a memorial to him. The Palliser baronetcy passed to his great-nephew Hugh Palliser Walters who assumed by Royal Licence dated 18 January 1798 the surname and arms of Palliser. Palliser's illegitimate son George Thomas inherited the estate of the Vache.

Hugh Palliser (Public Domain)

Back at Thicket, Nicholas turned his attention to his estate full time. It is not known if the disgrace of the court martial followed him back to the area, or what the effect was on himself personally. In 1743 Nicholas undid the entail on the Thicket Priory Estate set up by the trusts his father Humphrey Robinson entered into as discussed previously, and converted it to a fee simple. He then made provision for his sisters, Mary, who married Hugh Palliser, and Rebecca, who married Jacob Custobody.

Nicholas Robinson then made his will, dated 16 December 1752, in which he appointed his 'wellbeloved and trusty friends' Edward Wormley of Rickall, Esq., George Coulson of Skipwith, Esq., John Herbert of Selby, apothecary, and Henry Waite [senior] of York, Gent., as his executors. He bequeathed to his 'housekeeper' Mrs. Sarah Brearer a farm called Low Hall, and 'two mares the first one called Black Bess and the other Jipsey and two milk cows and furniture for two rooms and a kitchen and those such as my said trustees shall think proper to set out'. The Low Hall farm, after the death of the housekeeper, together with all his other 'real estate whatsoever at Thickett Cotingwith Thorganby Lofsam and Bedford in Holderness or elsewhere in the county of York' to his natural daughter, Sarah Robinson, otherwise Brearer, but upon condition that she and the heirs lawfully born of her body, take the surname Robinson. If Sarah had no heirs, then the estate would descend to his nephew, Captain Hugh Palliser and his heirs, but again, on condition that the heirs take the surname Robinson, and so on to his nephew the Rev. Jacob Custobody, then another nephew Henry Custobody, all with the same condition of the heirs taking the surname Robinson. If none of all his relatives named produced any heirs, then the entire estate would descend to his trustees to use as a rest home for four retired senior captains of His Majesty's Navy, but only if they reside there for eight months of the year, or else lose their benefit. All the rest of his goods and chattels he left to his natural daughter, Sarah. His executors were to receive all rents and profits from the estate for the maintenance and education of Sarah until she reached the age of 21 years, or married, and ordered that Sarah should abide by the advice and direction of the executors, particularly in any choice of suitor.

Nicholas then set up a marriage settlement, 30 December 1752, for his 'natural daughter, Sarah Robinson, otherwise Brearer', using the same properties as in the entail he had undone earlier, i.e. the manor of West Cottingwith cum Thorganby; Thicket Priory; Thicket Hall Farm; seven farms and tenements in West Cottingwith, Thorganby and Wheldrake; a messuage in York; land in Holderness; and a farm at Barnsley. The settlement was made prior to the intended marriage of Sarah to Henry Waite junior, the son of Henry Waite senior, a renowned lawyer of York and a very good and trusted friend and executor of Nicholas Robinson. The marriage of Sarah and Henry Waite junior took place on 2 January 1753 at Thorganby, by licence, stating that both the bride and groom were aged 18 years of age. The *London Magazine* and *The Gentleman's Magazine* both reported the marriage, and also gave the enormous sum of £25,000 as the value of this marriage!

Having survived to see his natural daughter married, Nicholas died and was buried 22 March 1753, at St. Mary Bishophill Senior, York. Probate of his will was granted in London at the Prerogative Court of Canterbury, dated 8 March 1754, with the administration being granted to one of the executors, Henry Waite [senior], saving the right of the other executors. Nicholas evidently had not the time, or perhaps the health, to update his will, as he died just a few weeks after Sarah's marriage.

Henry Waite *Robinson* and Sarah Robinson, alias Brearer

Nine months after their marriage Henry Waite junior and Sarah gave birth to twins, Henry and Nicholas Waite, but Henry died in infancy.

It is not known when Henry Waite first took on the name 'Henry Waite Robinson' following his marriage, but he was certainly using it from November 1758, when he took the first steps in divesting himself of the Thicket Priory Estate, when he placed a lease of a part of the estate, to lead to a release, in the hands of Lenyns Boldero, an attorney of Staples Inn in London, used frequently by the solicitors of York to plead cases in the Court of Common Pleas in London. This was a Common Recovery, a legal device to break an entail and convert an entailed property to a fee simple, or freehold with no encumbrances, and he recovered the estate later the same month. In June 1760 Henry placed the immediate Thicket Priory Estate in the hands of a trustee, a John Burton of York, doctor in physic, to create a new entail, which provided for the use of the Thicket Priory Estate to Henry Waite Robinson and Sarah his wife, for their lives, and after to the use of their son and sons in seniority, and for want of male heirs to the daughter or daughters, share and share alike. The entail also provided for the maintenance and education of any of their children being minors at the time of their decease.

The immediate estate at this time consisted of: Thicket Priory, Paddock; Thicket Hall with Ewe Close, Shop Garth, Coney Close, Sycomb Close, Far Park Close, the croft adjoining the house, High Close, Bainton Close, Far and Near Whin Closes, Lee Close, Acron Close, Stoop Close, New Park Close, and Wheldrake Ings; messuage Far Closes, 2 West Closes, Derwent Lands or Cow Pasture; messuage, Hill Close, Ellar Close, Garth Close with the Lane adjoining; with messuages (tenants named) and specified parcels in the fields and meadows of Thorganby and West Cottingwith. Land at Bedford in Holderness (Beeford?). The immediate estate did not include the manor of Cottingwith cum Thorganby, which was purchased by Emanuel Jefferson on 3 June 1760.

Henry Waite Robinson died and was buried at Wheldrake, 27 April 1799, leaving a will which was probated the following month. The immediate Thicket Priory Estate then passed to his eldest son, the Reverend Nicholas Waite Robinson, and to John Burton (the son of the John Burton, trustee in 1760). The brothers of the Reverend Nicholas all released their claims in 1801.

The Reverend Nicholas then severed all connection with the Thicket Priory Estate in April 1803, when he conveyed the immediate Thicket Priory Estate to Joseph Dunnington.

The Jefferson Family

The Jefferson family was a prosperous land-owning family in Hook, in the West Riding parish of Snaith. In the late seventeenth and early eighteenth century, two brothers, Joshua and Robert Jefferson, were particularly active.

Joshua and Robert Jefferson I

The elder brother, Joshua, died in October 1721 and his will reveals he had no children, instead leaving bequests to his niece Ann Gaythorn, brother Robert and his three children, David, Emanuel and Abigail. Robert Jefferson I eventually settled in Howden, and married Elizabeth Battell there in September 1693. Some of their children died young, but the three children who survived into adulthood were David, the son and heir, Emanuel, and Abigail, who married a Mr George Coates.

Emanuel Jefferson

Emanuel Jefferson was baptised 25 January 1703 at Howden parish church. He first occurs as an adult in January 1727 when he was left a house and land by his maternal uncle, William Battell of Selby. He then appears over the next 22 years increasing his land holdings. In October 1745 he first appears in relation to the Robinson family when he purchased two messuages in Selby and Howden from Richard Robinson and his wife Sarah, and with the Dunnington family when on 1 May 1749 he leased three farms and a cottage with various lands to David Jefferson of Hook, and John Dunnington of Thorganby. It was no mere coincidence that David Jefferson was Emanuel Jefferson's elder brother, and likewise John Dunnington was Eleanor Dunnington's elder brother, as just ten days later Emanuel Jefferson and Eleanor Dunnington were married. They had married by licence, which was obtained 10 May, with Emanuel taking great liberties with reporting his age as 35 (when in fact he was 45). Eleanor's age was given as 26. The following day they were married at Bishopthorpe.

Emanuel and Eleanor had four children; the first two, William and Ellin, both died young, while Robert, the son and heir, and Elizabeth, both reached adulthood.

Emanuel continued to improve his landholdings over the next twenty years. In November 1760 he bought the manor of Cottingwith cum Thorganby with 5 messuages, barns, stables and orchards, 160ac. land, 100ac. each of meadow, pasture, furze and heath, and moor, pasture for 27 beasts and rents of £1 1s. 2d., all in West Cottingwith and Thorganby, from Henry Waite Robinson. Emanuel had no great love for his estate in West Cottingwith and Thorganby; his heart was firmly with Howden. In 1764 the minister of Thorganby complained to Archbishop Drummond, during his visitation of the Diocese: 'There is a private school in my parish endowed with 40s. per annum, which was left by Thomas Dunnington of this parish 30 years since, and which has been regularly paid to the curate, who is the schoolmaster, by Emanuel Jefferson, Esq. of Howden, to Michaelmas 1754, and since that time he has never paid it, and will give no reason why he will not pay it'. The minister also complained about payments to alms-houses: 'There is 4s. 6d. paid out of a close called Isaac's Close belonging to Emanuel Jefferson Esq. of Howden which has not been paid since the year 1750'. Throughout all this time Emanuel held local public office, as a Justice of the Peace.

In February 1764, Emanuel's wife, Eleanor, died at the relatively young age of 41, and Emanuel died 5 years later, 29 December 1769; both were buried in the parish church of Howden.

Emanuel had drawn up his will 23 February 1761 and died 29 Dec 1769. He was buried at Howden, with the entry in the parish register describing him as 'Justice of ye Peace'. In his will Emanuel left some land to his beloved wife Eleanor, for her widowhood, but the bulk of his estate, both real and personal, he left to his son, Robert, who was a minor at the time of the making of the will. He left the tuition of Robert to his wife, and allowed Robert to choose his guardians himself when he reached the age of sixteen years. Eleanor died some three years after the making of the will, and Emanuel did not update his will to reflect this, especially after Emanuel named his wife as the sole executor of his will. The will was probated 16 January 1770, but it is curious that the will was probated at all, as in the case of sole executor dying before the testator, the will becomes invalid, and a simple administration should have taken place, with the will annexed, but as Robert was the residual beneficiary it would have been him that administration would normally have been awarded to anyway.

Robert Jefferson II

Emanuel's son and heir, whom we must now designate Robert Jefferson II, was even more active in improving his landowning position, though the majority of these were in the Howden area. He leased the Bishop's Manor House (also known as Hall Garth) in Howden in February 1777 and renewed the lease in 1784, 1791 and 1805. If he lived personally in this grand house then he lived in style.

Robert's land dealings in the Thorganby and West Cottingwith area consisted primarily of renewing or regranting leases of West Cottingwith Farm, and Low Hall in Thorganby but does appear to have increased his landholdings there just prior to his death. Surveys of his lands, with valuations, were conducted in 1777 and again in 1807.

The site of Thicket Priory was used primarily at this time merely for hunting and fishing. In 1796-1798 the appointment of a gamekeeper was recorded in the local newspapers in compliance with the Stamp Duty Acts, which were charged on the issuance of gamekeepers' licences. The returns for those years were made by the Deputy Clerk of the Peace for the East Riding, when William Waite was listed as gamekeeper, covering the manors of 'Thickett Priory, West Cottingwith, and a moiety of East Cottingwith.' In each case the appointment was recorded as having been made by Henry Waite Robinson and Robert Jefferson.

Robert Jefferson II made one major impact as the principal landowner in Thorganby and West Cottingwith. He petitioned Parliament in February 1810 for a Private Act to enclose the commons and wastes of the parish and extinguish the common rights to pasture, woodland and other rights. The petition was countersigned by all the major landowners in the parish, and was opposed by a few 'voices' that did not wish to relinquish these rights. However, the bill was eventually passed 4 May, receiving the Royal Assent 2 June 1810.

Robert never married, dying without lawful issue at the age of 55, and was buried at Howden 31 July 1811. He had made his will 15 January 1803 which passed probate 18 February 1812.

He left all his real estate to his friend John Dunnington the elder, of Thorganby, for life, as trustee, then to John Dunnington the younger, but conditional upon them adopting the surname 'Jefferson'. The trust was charged with the payments of several life annuities to relatives, friends and servants. He also provided to the resident minister of Howden and his successors, '20 guineas annually for teaching 12 poor boys of Howden in the Grammar School there in reading writing and arithmetic, and 5 guineas annually for preaching a sermon on the anniversary of his burial.' He also left the churchwardens and overseers of the poor of Howden £10 on 24 December annually, for coals to be distributed amongst the poor of Howden.

Additionally, he left to the resident minister of West Cottingwith or Thorganby and his successors '10 guineas to teach 8 children of the tenants of the estates in reading writing and arithmetic', and also left to the churchwardens and overseers of the poor of West Cottingwith or Thorganby £6 on 24 December annually, for coals to be distributed amongst the poor of West Cottingwith. He asked his executors to ensure that he was buried in Howden, as near to his father's grave as possible. A memorial to his memory was erected in Howden Minster, in the west wall of the south transcept:

Sacred to the Memory
of
Robert Jefferson Esquire,
of Howden in the East Riding
of the County of York,
Formerly a Captain in His Majesty's
Royal Regiment of Horse Guards blue,
Who died on the 28th of July 1811,
Aged 55 years;
And was interred in a Vault near this place

Ingenuous, affable and inoffensive,
Faithfull to his Friends;
Liberal to his Tenantry;
Benevolent towards Mankind;
Such was Robert Jefferson

To heal the Infirmaties of the Body;
To mitigate the Maladies of the Mind;
To diffuse Education among the Poor;
To promote agricultural Industry;
Were, in his Estimation, Virtues
Which adorn the Christian Character.

Having provided amply for his Relations,
He testified his Sense of these Dutie,
By the following liberal Bequests:

To the Infirmary at York, £500:
To the Asylum for Lunatics at York, £500:
To the School at Howden annually, £21:
To the School at West Cottingwith & Thorganby annually, £6:
To his Tenants Leases for their Lives
Of the Land in their Occupation
At the Rents, upon the Conditions
Prevailing at the time of his Decease

"Reader! Imitate his Examples"
"Be Mercifull after thy Power"

The memorial was described in a contemporary newspaper thus:

'Two emblematic figures, as large as natural life, representing Faith and Charity, were sculptured in the purest white marble; the latter unveiled an urn, after the antique, whilst the former inscribed the name of the deceased upon its centre. Charity at the same time embraces her child sleeping on her bosom, and with a countenance expressive of tender solicitude watches the occupation of Faith.'

The Dunnington Family

The Dunnington or 'de Dunnington' family, as the name suggests, originated in the village of Dunnington, six miles east of York, but eventually spread throughout the East Riding and beyond. A John Dunnington was a lessee of Turnham Hall in Hemingbrough in the early seventeenth century with his wife Frances, but as they were Recusants she was fined in 1608, and his tenancy was estreated in 1612.

Thomas Dunnington senior and junior

Thomas Dunnington senior and junior occur in Thorganby from at least 1699 when they were involved in a mortgage on an earlier conveyance of 22 acres called Parke Close in Thorganby. More property in Thorganby was acquired 1703-1707 by Thomas Dunnington, but it is not clear whether this was by Thomas Dunnington senior or junior. Thomas Dunnington senior died and was buried 11 June 1710, and the acquisition of further land after this year was now unambiguous when it referred to Thomas Dunnington, who continued to further the family's acquisitions of property in the parishes of Thorganby and Bubwith until his death and burial at Thorganby 12 October 1733.

Thomas Dunnington made his will 9 October 1733 and was probated at the Prerogative Court of York in April 1734. The will mentions his wife, Ellin (Eleanor), eldest son John, and younger son William, and daughter Ellen (Eleanor) and grandson Thomas, who was the schoolmaster at Thorganby. The lands mentioned included holdings in Thorganby, West Cottingwith, Bubwith, Selby, Barlby, Skipwith and Wheldrake. He left Hesslewood House in West Cottingwith to trustees as a schoolhouse for the schoolmaster, and successive schoolmasters, and 40s. per annum.

Unfortunately his second son, William, died a young man, being buried at Thorganby, 27 October 1746, aged just 21 years. Eleanor, the widow of Thomas, died and was also buried at Thorganby, 3 March 1757.

Eleanor, the daughter of Thomas, married Emanuel Jefferson 11 May 1749, as we have seen in the Emanuel Jefferson sub-section previously.

John Dunnington senior and junior

The eldest son of Thomas, John Dunnington, married Dorothy Tomlinson 29 May 1759 at Brayton by licence (with the consent of her mother). They had seven children: sons John (the eldest), Thomas, William and Joseph; and daughters Elizabeth, Dorothy and Jane, but Elizabeth and Dorothy both died in infancy. The eldest, John Dunnington, was born illegitimate, being born a few weeks before his parents' marriage.

John Dunnington senior made little impact on the family's holdings in the area, but he did rebuild the schoolhouse, which provided free education for more than half of the children in the area, while his younger brother Thomas acted as schoolmaster there. John also paid 10s. annually for an anniversary sermon at Hemingbrough. John Dunnington senior died 26 June 1810 and was buried in the chancel of Thorganby church. He was 85 years of age and died of 'natural decay'. He left a will dated 18 December 1807, in which he left £200 each to his sons Thomas, William and Joseph, and £1,000 each to his daughters Dorothy and Jane. All the rest of his estate, real and personal, he left to his eldest son John, whom he made his sole executor. The will also contained the reason for not giving his sons Thomas, William and Joseph, a larger legacy in his will, which was that he had previously given them what he intended and thought a fair proportion of his property. The will was probated 22 September 1810.

John Dunnington junior never married but did increase the family holdings. The owner of the manor of Thorganby in 1801 was Thomas Bradford who broke up the manor and sold it in lots. The largest lot was the Hall House and 243 acres which was bought by John Dunnington junior in 1802. The manorial rights and 69 acres were bought by Thomas Kendall in 1810 and he in turn sold them to John Dunnington (now John Dunnington-Jefferson) in 1815.

Change of Name

In compliance with the will of Robert Jefferson discussed previously, John Dunnington applied for a Royal Licence to add the name 'Jefferson' to his own. The licence was granted 29 January 1812 and was published in *The London Gazette*:

> His Royal Highness the Prince Regent, in the name and on the behalf of His Majesty, hath also been graciously pleased to give and grant unto John Dunnington, of Thorganby, in the county of York, Esquire, His Majesty's royal licence and authority, that he, and his issue, when they shall respectively be in the actual possession of certain real estates under the last will and testament of Robert Jefferson, late of Howden, in the said county, Esquire, deceased, and in compliance with an injunction therein contained, may use and take the surname of Jefferson in addition to that of Dunnington, provided that the said royal concession and declaration be recorded in His Majesty's College of Arms.

The London Gazette, 1 February 1812, Issue 16570, p. 226

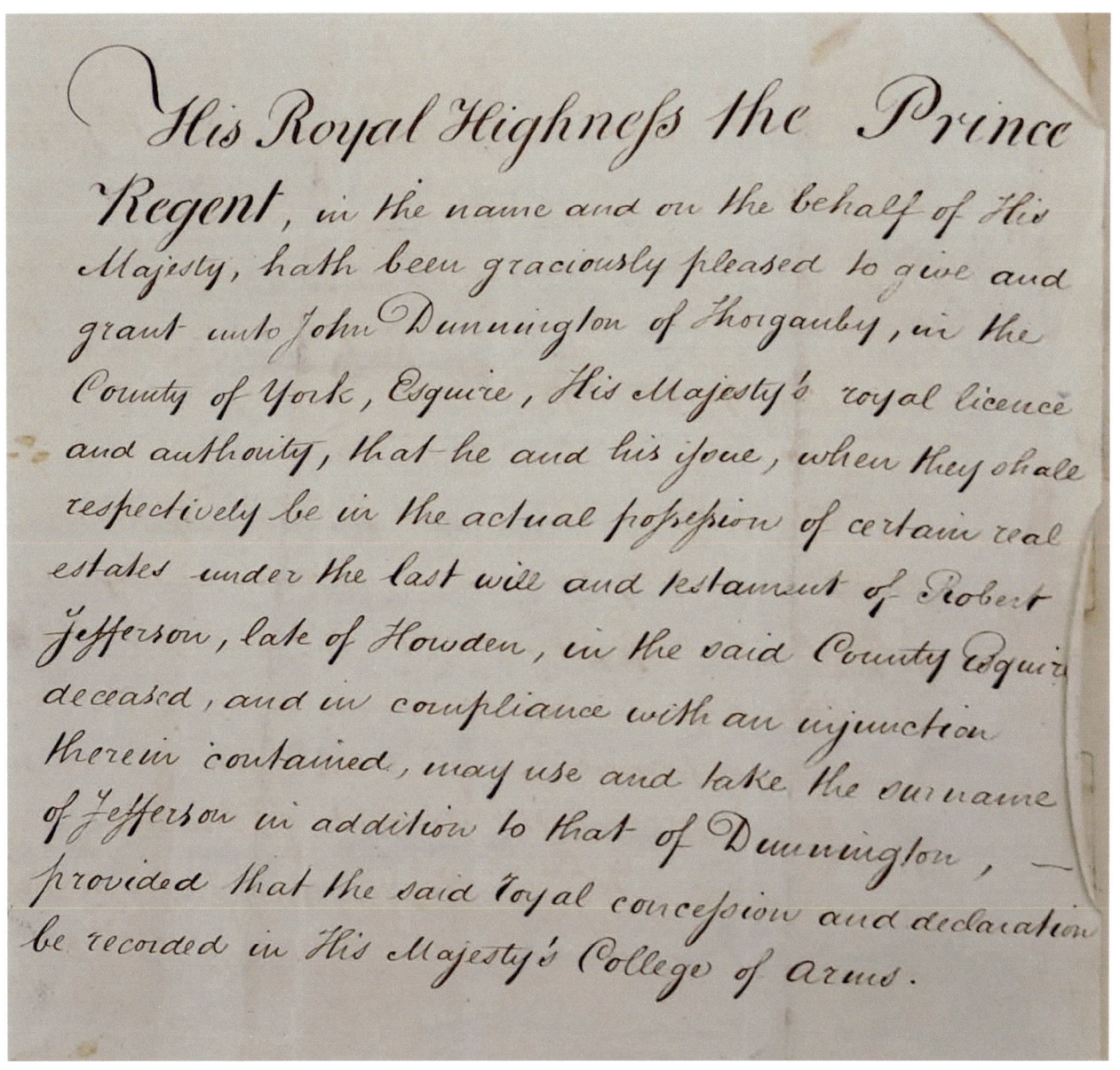

Letter from the Prince Regent to John Dunnington, from the personal archives of the Dunnington-Jefferson Family

His Royal Highness the, Prince Regent, in the name and on the behalf of His Majesty, hath also been graciously pleased to give and grant unto John Dunnington, of Thorganby, in the county of York, Esquire, His Majesty's royal licence and authority, that he, and his issue, when they shall respectively be in the actual possession of certain real estates under the last will and testament of Robert Jefferson, late of Howden, in the said county, Esquire, deceased, and in compliance with an injunction therein contained, may use and take the surname of Jefferson in addition to that of Dunnington, provided that the said royal concession and declaration be recorded in His Majesty's College of Arms.

The above letter was accompanied by a warrant, addressed to Charles, Duke of Norfolk, Earl Marshal of England, signed by King George III, and bearing the royal seal. The warrant noted that the petitioner, John Dunnington, had petitioned for a royal licence to add the surname of Jefferson to his own, reciting the wishes expressed under the will of Robert Jefferson, and that the king, by his special favour had granted his petition, but upon condition that the petitioner take a coat of arms, issued and recorded by the College of Arms. The warrant was duly recorded in the College of Arms 11 February 1812.

John Dunnington-Jefferson

Following the change of name John Dunnington-Jefferson continued to improve the family finances. He loaned money to other would-be landholders in the area, and in 1817 he loaned £2,000 to John Dyson, for the use of Benjamin Halley to purchase lands in Thorganby, and the premises purchased were mortgaged to John.

In 1822 John decided to rebuild Thorganby Hall. The original Thorganby Hall was probably the 'Hall House' sold in 1802 by Thomas Bradford to John Dunnington.

John Dunnington-Jefferson, in his old age, began to think of his mortality and his familial affairs. He sold a mansion house he owned in Loddon, co. Norfolk, to his brother Thomas in April 1827, and in January 1835 he surrendered to Thomas the land known as Butt Field Close of 5 acres.

John Dunnington-Jefferson of Thorganby Hall died in 1840 and was buried 22 September at Thorganby. He had made a will, probated at the Prerogative Court of York, with an estate valued at £35,000, an enormous sum in those days, and worth over three million pounds by today's standards.

He left his mansion house, Thorganby Hall, to his brother Thomas Dunnington of Ardwick in the parish of Manchester and his sister Jane Dunnington of Thorganby, for life. He also left them all his goods and chattels, after payment of his just debts, funeral expenses, probate charges, and the payment of his legacies, equally, forever.

His brother and sister, Thomas and Jane, continued to live at Thorganby Hall.

The estate was inherited by John's nephew, Joseph Dunnington junior, son of John's brother, Joseph Dunnington senior who had married Mary Toutill in 1805.

Joseph Dunnington junior went to school in Manchester and went on to attend St. John's, Cambridge, in 1825, gaining his BA in 1830 and his MA in 1833. He was ordained deacon in 1831 and priest in 1832, becoming vicar of Thorganby the same year.

Joseph junior married Anna Mervynia Vavasour, eldest daughter of Lieutenant General Sir Henry Maghull Mervin Vavasour, 2nd Bart. of the Horse Grenadier Guards, by Anne Vavasour, eldest daughter of William Vavasour of Dublin, LLD, by licence at Monkstown near Dublin, 23 May 1839. Sir Henry had died in 1838, and Anna was probably with her recently widowed mother in Dublin, possibly explaining why she and Joseph had married in the nearby affluent suburb of Monkstown.

Following the return to Thicket Priory, the Rev. Joseph obtained a licence from the Archbishop of York in 1839 to settle his ecclesiastical residence at Thicket Priory, instead of the usual curate's house, as the curate's house was considered unfit for the Rev. Joseph's station in life. The following year the happy couple had their first child, a daughter, Mervynia, who was baptised at Thorganby, 29 November 1840.

Like his uncle, in order to inherit the estate, Joseph also underwent a change of name, assuming the surname of Jefferson by Royal Licence in 1841.

Whitehall, May 21, 1841.
The Queen has been pleased to grant unto
Joseph Dunnington, of Thicket Priory, in the county
of York, Clerk, Master of Arts, Her Majesty's royal
licence and authority, that he and his issue may,
out of grateful respect for the memory of Robert
Jefferson, late of Howden, in the said county, Esq.
deceased, take and henceforth use the surname of
Jefferson, in addition to and after that of Dunnington, and also bear the arms of
Jefferson quarterly,
in the first quarter, with his own family arms;
such arms being first duly exemplified according

to the laws of arms, and recorded in the Heralds'
Office, otherwise the said royal licence and permission to be void and of none
effect:
And also to command, that the said royal concession and declaration be recorded
in Her Majesty's College of Arms.

It is not clear from the above announcement whether the quartering of arms and their registration at the College of Arms was a condition of the granting of the Royal Licence to effect the change of name, or whether the application made by Joseph for a change of name also included a request for a coat of arms. As the announcement makes clear that the failure to exemplify the arms in the Herald's Office would void the Royal Licence, it would appear that the former is the case.

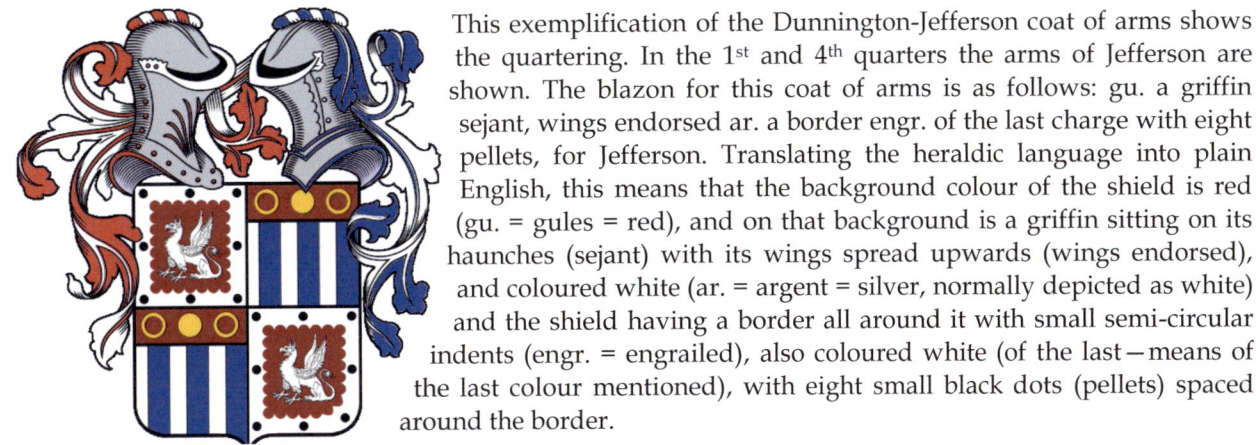

This exemplification of the Dunnington-Jefferson coat of arms shows the quartering. In the 1st and 4th quarters the arms of Jefferson are shown. The blazon for this coat of arms is as follows: gu. a griffin sejant, wings endorsed ar. a border engr. of the last charge with eight pellets, for Jefferson. Translating the heraldic language into plain English, this means that the background colour of the shield is red (gu. = gules = red), and on that background is a griffin sitting on its haunches (sejant) with its wings spread upwards (wings endorsed), and coloured white (ar. = argent = silver, normally depicted as white) and the shield having a border all around it with small semi-circular indents (engr. = engrailed), also coloured white (of the last – means of the last colour mentioned), with eight small black dots (pellets) spaced around the border.

Dunnington-Jefferson Arms

In the 2nd and 3rd quarters the arms of Dunnington are shown. The blazon for this coat of arms is as follows: paly of six ar. and az. on a chief gu. a bezant between two annulets or, for Dunnington. In plain English this means that the shield is divided into six vertical bars of equal width (paly of six), with the first being coloured white (ar. = argent = silver = white), and the next coloured blue (az. = azure = blue), alternatively. The shield is then divided again, having a separate top area (chief) coloured red (gu. = gules = red), with a bezant (a gold coin, common in the Holy Land during the Crusades), depicted as a solid yellow disc), between two rings of yellow (annulets).

I cannot find any reference to a member of either of the East Riding Jefferson or Dunnington families ever having been granted a coat of arms prior to this registration in the Heralds' College, and I suspect that these two coats, quartered, were designed by the College, rather than by the family. Some aspects of the coats are discernable though.

The Dunnington coat of arms is very similar to the arms of the Donnington family (from a completely unrelated village of that name, and nothing to do with the village of Dunnington, just east of York where 'our' Dunnington family hails from). The arms have been 'differenced' slightly in that the arms of the Donnington family have three bezants in chief, whereas the arms of the Dunnington family have had two of these bezants turned into annulets, which are usually used in heraldry as a difference mark to denote a fifth son.

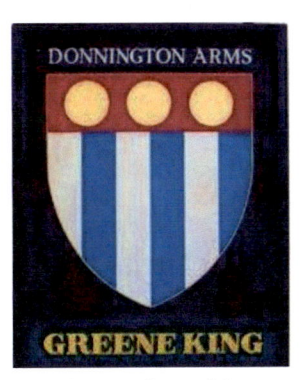

Donnington Coat of Arms

Thicket and Ellerton Estate Buildings

In February 1535/6 Parliament passed 'The Suppression of Religious Houses Act' or the 'Act for the Dissolution of the Lesser Monasteries', as it was known, and following the Act Thicket Priory was visited by the commissioners, Leonard Beckwith and Hugh Fuller, who undertook an inventory of all movable and immovable assets. The commissioners then confiscated nearly all the movable assets; the only things they left at this point were the bells and lead, which were placed in the custody of a servant of the Royal Household, William Wytheham (Wytham, Witham).

However, Thicket Priory was not dissolved immediately and survived until it was surrendered, which occurred 27 August 1539. The following February, 1539/40, the site of Thicket Priory, its demesne and land were leased to William Wytham.

The fate of the bells and lead was never alluded to directly, but it would appear that at some point William Witham had passed them to the commissioners, as in 1546 the former commissioner, Leonard Beckwith, who was now Comptroller of Boulogne, wrote to Sir William Paget, one of the two Principal Secretaries and chancellor of the Duchy of Lancaster, beseeching him:

> *Please get me licence to come into England for a time, both to order my house and things in Yorkshire, for which at coming to Court I had no leisure, and because I have lead, bell metal and evidences of the King's, and no warrant to whom to deliver them.*
> *Bulloigne, 27 Nov. 1546.*

It was common at this time to plunder anything of value from the dissolved abbeys, monasteries and priories that had been subsequently leased out or sold. The natural decay following the removal of the lead from the main religious buildings, and the plunder of the timbers and bricks or stone from those buildings for the repair of the remaining farm buildings, of which Thicket Priory had a number, led to a gradual ruination. Only the religious buildings suffered this way, to prevent any later attempt to resurrect them; the farm buildings were left intact in order to raise as much income from their lease or sale. The Royal Commission that the commissioners received was quite explicit in this regard, as John Freman, one of Cromwell's deputies wrote to his master in August 1539:

> *The King's commission commands me to pull down to the ground all the walls of the churches, steeples, &c., leaving only houses necessary for a farmer. "Sir, there be more of great houses in Lincolnshire than be in England beside suppressed of their values, with thick walls, and most part of them vawtid, and few byars of other stone, glasse or slatt which might help the charges of plokyng down of them. "To follow the commission will cost the King 1,000l. at least within the shire. Means first to take down the bells and lead, which will bring 6,000 or 7,000 marks, then pull down the roofs, battlements, and stairs, letting the walls stand" and charge some with them as a quarry of stone to make sales of," unless Cromwell think better otherwise. Valdey, 7 Aug.*

Wytham was to hold his lease until 3 April 1542, when John Aske, the patron of Thicket at the Dissolution, acquired it in fee simple, along with other properties in Yorkshire, in exchange for his manors in Sussex. A detailed description of the lands that John Aske acquired from the king in this exchange exists, in the records of the Court of Augmentations, and the entry for the trees about The Scyte and demesnes of the late priory of Thyckhed in the seid countie (of Yorks) were described as follows:

> *The trees growing aboute the scytuacion of the seid late pryorye and fences and in hedges inclosyng landes perteynyng to the same wyll barely suffyce for tymber to repayre the houses standyng uppon the scyte of the seid late pryorye and fences and to mayntane the hedges and fences aboute the same therfore not val.*

The full Patent Roll entry for this exchange also gives more detail for the Thicket Priory part of the exchange, and includes the information that the site and demesnes of Thicket included a windmill, and named closes, as listed in the section 'The Aftermath of the Dissolution'.

The Aske family never resided in Thorganby or West Cottingwith. They had their mansion in Aughton which had been in the family for generations and simply leased the site of Thicket Priory to tenants. The *Inquisitions Post Mortem* of the successive Aske heirs show that the only 'capital messuage' they held in the area was Cottingwith Grange, the former grange of Ellerton Priory. There was no capital messuage in Thicket noted in the IPMs.

When John Aske sold the sites of Thicket and Ellerton priories to John Robinson in 1596, the Robinson family likewise simply leased out the site of Thicket Priory to tenants, and continued to reside in London. It was not until a descendent, Humphrey Robinson, acquired the Thicket Priory Estate in 1622 from his father Henry Robinson that we hear of the first of this Robinson family to be actually resident at Thicket Priory, as in Humphrey's will dated 5 October 1626 he explicitly says he is "of Thicket Priory". However, the sale from

Henry Robinson to his son Humphrey in 1622 does not mention any capital messuage, only 'the site of the late Priory of Thickhead and 8 messuages and 8 cottages'. It is possible that Humphrey and his family were living in one of the smaller messuages at Thicket while a capital messuage was being built, or more likely, at Cottingwith Grange.

Certainly before 1656 a capital messuage had been built at Thicket, as Richard Robinson mentioned it in the marriage settlement of his younger son, Richard Robinson junior, on his upcoming marriage to Jane, daughter of John Ayckroyd of Foggathorpe, in November 1656. This was a very substantial house, recorded as having 10 hearths in the Hearth Tax returns of Lady Day 1672.

Cottingwith Grange had been used by Ellerton Priory, prior to its dissolution, as its *locum* in the Ouse and Derwent area, with its farmer being responsible for collecting rents, tithes and other dues on behalf of the priory.

John Herbert had bought the goods and chattels of the priory at the Dissolution in 1539, and acquired the lease of the entire site in March 1540. The title in the site was sold by the Crown to John Aske of Aughton on 1 April 1542, and Ellerton Priory, along with its capital messuage of Cottingwith Grange, remained with the Aske family until another John Aske sold it to John Robinson in 1596.

In John Robinson's will 12 July 1599, he mentions that he has previously sold 'the lordship of Dighton, the monasterie of Ellerton, the priorie of Thickhed and Cottingwith Graunge, with other landes in Cottingwithe and Thurgamby' to his sons Henry and Arthur. It is clear that these properties were not sold jointly and severally. Arthur was sold the manor of Deighton, and Henry the remainder, which included Cottingwith Grange.

As we have seen in the section, The Robinson Family, Henry Robinson sold the site of the late priory of Ellerton, with lands in Ellerton, Aughton, East Cottingwith, West Cottingwith and Thorganby to Sir Robert Ducie during the Hilary Term of 1621/2; and the site of the priory of Thickhead with dwellings and land in Thickhead, West Cottingwith, Thorganby and Wheldrake, to his nephew Humphrey Robinson, son of his brother John Robinson junior, during the Michaelmas Term of 1622.

Later, Humphrey Robinson's son, Richard Robinson senior, purchased the Ducie dwellings and lands in West Cottingwith and Thorganby in June–August 1659, reuniting the Thicket Priory Estate in Wheldrake, West Cottingwith and Thorganby once again.

In 1672 Richard senior placed Cottingwith Grange, along with three cottages and land in West Cottingwith and a messuage in Thorganby, in trust, for his own use for life, then to his wife Elizabeth for life in lieu of dower, and then to son and heir Richard Robinson junior, for life, with remainder to Humphrey Robinson son and heir of Richard Robinson junior.

No references to Cottingwith Grange appear after 1672, and in the Hearth Tax Returns of 1675 there is only one capital messuage in West Cottingwith, containing 10 hearths, and that can only have been the rebuilt Thicket Priory II, sometimes known as Thicket Hall. Several small farms have two hearths, suggesting that Cottingwith Grange became unfit for use shortly after 1672, being over 134 years old at least since it was listed in the Dissolution documents of Ellerton Priory.

The rebuilt Thicket Priory II was referred to as the 'Mansion House in Thickhead' in another marriage settlement in June 1690, and is mentioned again in July 1721 when Humphrey Robinson senior made a settlement to secure the portions for his children, Henry, Nicholas and Rebecca Robinson, the younger brothers and sister of Humphrey Robinson junior. A drawing of this house is shown in Samuel Buck's Yorkshire Sketchbook, dated 1720, now held at the British Library, Department of Manuscripts, where it is simply described as 'The South West Prospect of Thicket, The seat of Humph. Robinson Esq'.

Sketch of 'Thicket', from Samuel Buck's Yorkshire Sketchbook (stables, coachhouse, dovecote and main house)

Thicket Priory II (Thicket Hall) – A Reconstruction

The 'Reconstruction of Thicket Priory II' above was created using the sketch of Thicket by Samuel Buck, the architectural norms of the period and the remains of the 'Robinson House' still visible today in the grounds of the present Thicket Priory.

The Remains of Thicket Priory II (Thicket Hall),
(Rear-left corner, with stone quoins, and showing the windows of basement rooms, probably the kitchens)

In 1803 Nicholas Waite Robinson put Thicket Hall up for sale, the agents being Messrs. Kent, Claridge, and Pearce of Craig's Court, Charing Cross, London. The 'Descriptive Particular' they issued for this sale provided a description of the property, its outbuildings, farmhouse and land.

> The MANSION HOUSE, called THICKET HALL, is an Edifice of Three Stories, Brick and Tile, and in Part covered with Lead; is beautifully situated in one of the most fertile Parts of the County of York, on the Banks of the River Darwent; well Planted, and highly Ornamented by Timber, and might, at a very easy Expence afford Accomodation for a large Family, having a Hall, spacious Rooms, double Staircase, good Cellarage, detached Kitchen, Brew-house, Dairy, and all other useful and convenient Offices.
>
> A good Farm House, Cottage, large Barns, Dove House covered with Lead; Horse Mill, open Barns, excellent Stabling and Coach Houses, Farm Stable, Beast House, Ox Stalls, Cow Houses, Cart House, very large and extensive Granaries, Pig Sties, and Sheds for Cattle, Dog Kennel, and Boiling House, all Brick and Tile, substantially Built upon an extensive Scale. Kitchen Garden walled in; and Fish Ponds: Together with the following Pieces and Parcels of rich Inclosed Arable, Meadow, and Pasture LAND, all contiguous to the said Mansion House; the Soil of a superior Quality, and in a high state of Cultivation, now in the Occuption of Mr. William Jubb.

The above description was then followed by a listing of all the pieces of land, togther with their respective tenants, and a note that the whole estate was subject to a yearly Land Tax to West Cottingwith of £13 6s. 0d.

From 1769–1843 the house was usually referred to as Thicket Hall. However, in the 1841 census it was referred to once more as Thicket Priory, and it was occupied by Joseph Dunnington, aged 30, with his wife Anna, aged 25, and their baby daughter Mavenia (*sic*), along with 7 servants.

Thorganby Hall, originally the 'Hall House' sold in 1802 by Thomas Bradford to John Dunnington, was rebuilt in 1822 by John Dunnington-Jefferson, who died and was buried 22 September 1840 at Thorganby.

The 1841 census lists Thomas Dunnington, aged 78, with wife Jane, aged 73, residing at Thorganby Hall, together with 4 servants, and in the 1851 census only Jane was left, aged 83, again with 4 servants. Jane was still living at Thorganby Hall in 1861, when she appears again on the census for that year, now aged 92, and still with her 4 servants. Jane died and was buried at Thorganby 26 March 1863, aged 95. The day before Jane was buried the house and farm were put up for rent and appeared in *The Yorkshire Gazette* edition of March 28, 1863.

> THORGANBY HALL AND FARM, EAST YORKSHIRE, TO BE LET, from Year to Year, and Entered on immediately. The House contains Breakfast, Dining, and Drawing Rooms, Offices, &c., on the Ground Floor, and above are good Bed Rooms and Servants Rooms. The Farm Buildings are modern and very excellent. The Farm is compact and truly desirable, and contains Upwards of Three Hundred Acres. A considerable quantity of it is very superior old Grass, capable of feeding Cattle of any size, and the remainder is of good quality. The River Dement runs contiguous to part of the Land, and the Parish Landing Place will enable a Tenant at a light expense to obtain Manure and send away his Produce. The Cliff Station on the Hull and Selby Railway is within Eight, and the Cliff Common Gate on the Selby and Market Weighton Line within Seven Miles. The Farm is to be Let solely on account of a recent death. It has been for more than a century occupied by the owners, and is in a good state of cultivation and in every way fit for immediate entry. The Hay, Straw, &c., can, if desired by a Tenant, be taken at a Valuation.
> To View, and for further Particulars, apply to Mr. BURLAND, Thorganby, near York.
> Thorganby 25th March, 1863.

The story of the third rebuilding of Thicket Priory in 1844 will be taken up in the next chapter, together with its subsequent history through the Victorian years, two World Wars, and how the priory came to be home to a sisterhood of nuns once again.

CHAPTER 3
Thicket Priory II to Thicket Priory III

The Building of Thicket Priory III – Sad News – Victorian Life at the Priory
Joseph John Dunnington-Jefferson – Tragic Event – Thicket Priory III for Rent

The Building of Thicket Priory III
In 1844 the Rev. Joseph Dunnington-Jefferson decided to have a new grand residence built, to replace the old Thicket Priory (Thicket Hall) of the Robinson family and embarked on an ambitious building project—a new Thicket Priory. The architect he employed for this prestigious project was none other than Edward Blore, notable for his works on Lambeth Palace, Buckingham Palace, Hampton Court Palace, Windsor Castle and many others.

Edward Blore

The Clerk of the Works for the building of Thicket Priory, Elliott Walter, kept meticulous accounts, but the bland numbers in the account books still revealed some interesting insights.

The on-site work began at the end of May, 1844. The men initially employed consisted of bricklayers, carpenters and labourers, but were joined by wood sawyers from the middle of June. The team of men was joined in early July by masons and stone sawyers, showing that the stonework was not cut and dressed off-site but rather on-site. In mid-July they were joined by a blacksmith and in mid-August by brickmakers. Some of the materials for the site arrived by river, particularly bricks and sand from Hull, via the Humber and lower reaches of the Derwent, and Malton stone from the upper reaches of the Derwent. The accounts recorded many payments for 'river dues'.

Blore came to Thicket twice before the on-site work began, on 13 October 1843, and 10 March 1844. He followed this up with journeys for meetings on 16 June, 2 July and 2 September through 1844.

The on-site workmen continued apace during 1845, and were eventually joined by plumbers and slaters in the May and plasterers in the August. From 18 April to 17 October a Mr. Robert Dryden appears on the payroll, who had been hired as foreman of the Clerk of the Works.

In 1847 we learn that Robert Dryden has taken over as the Clerk of the Works, though receiving 50s. per week as opposed to the 63s. per week received by his predecessor, Elliott Walter. By the end of 1847 the work was essentially complete. The only work listed during 1848 was for the fitting of the chapel, and designs for new lodges. Blore made his last visit to Thicket on 17 April. The cost for building the new Thicket Priory was close to £20,000.

Sad News

While the work on building the new Thicket Priory was going on, a terrible accident occurred. A newspaper of the day reported it thus:

> MELANCHOLY AND FATAL OCCURRENCE. --- An event in strict accordance with this heading occurred on Monday week, at the beautiful mansion which is now in the course of erection by the Rev. J. D. Jefferson, at Thicket Priory, in the East Riding of this county. On the morning of that day a promising young man named Benjamin Buckley, a bricklayer, was engaged at work on the top of the building, when owing to some unaccountable mishap his foot slipped, and he was precipitated to the foundation of the structure, a distance of 192 feet, and almost dashed to pieces. The unfortunate youth was taken up in a state of insensibility; but by medical assistance and proper nourishment he continued to breathe until the subsequent Wednesday, when death put a period to his sufferings. An inquest was held on Thursday at the County Hospital [public house], in Wheldrake, before John Wood, Esq., the coroner, and a respectable jury, when a verdict of 'accidental death' was returned. The deceased was a native of this town, and, what adds to the melancholy circumstance, was to have been married to a respectable young female at Wheldrake on the day on which his remains were consigned to the tomb.

During the construction of Thicket Priory, the Reverend Joseph also laid plans in 1846 for the rebuilding of Ellerton Priory, paying £695 to Simpson and Malone, stonemasons and carpenters of Hull, to carry out the work. The beautiful little church was completed and consecrated 26 April 1848 by the Archbishop of York.

But then, more sad news was to follow.

Mention has been made of the birth of Mervynia, the daughter of Joseph and Anna in 1840. The couple went on to have a further eight children: Caroline Emma, bap. 23 October 1842; Mary Campbell, bap. 1 December 1844; Joseph John, bapt. 21 December 1845; Henry Mervyn and Thomas, twin boys, bap. 22 January 1847; Theodosia, bap. 30 July 1848; Mervyn, bap. 31 March 1850; and Thomas Trafford, bap. 3 April 1853.

Unfortunately, tragedy struck the family, with the twin boys, Henry Mervyn and Thomas, dying as newborns, and they were buried together, 27 January 1847, just five days after their baptism; and Caroline

Emma, dying at the age of ten in a terrible accident at Scarborough, when she fell over the balustrades in the guest house where she was staying and was killed instantly.

Victorian Life at the Priory

The Reverend Joseph was an archetypal country gentleman. He was the perpetual curate of Thorganby, a canon of York Minster, a local magistrate, and the lord of several manors, including Thorganby, West Cottingwith, Bellasize, Eastrington, Gilberdyke, Harlethorpe, Newport and Goole.

Along with Thicket Priory and its 150-acre park he controlled 7,278 acres in the East Riding, producing an annual rental of £10,936, along with 533 acres in the West Riding, worth another £1,067. He also chaired many local charities and local action groups. As well as supporting the school in West Cottingwith, (originally set up by Thomas Dunnington in 1733), the Reverend also erected a free school and chapel in Newport which opened 18 April 1855, and was heavily involved in the erection of the new church in Fulford which opened in December 1866.

The Reverend's big passions were cattle breeding, amassing many awards for his short-horn cattle, and breeding pedigree horses which he bred at his Thicket Priory Stud Farm. He was also a member of the Royal Agricultural Society of England, and an active country sportsman, hosting many shoots, as well as fox-hunting and fishing expeditions.

To maintain his hunting rights on his estates, the Reverend employed several local men as gamekeepers, and unfortunately a nasty accident befell one of them. A Mr. Jacques, one of the Reverend's gamekeepers, was out shooting rabbits with his son, when the son accidently shot his father, the said Mr. Jacques, and 15 pieces of buckshot lodged in his shoulder. A newspaper of the day reported the accident and went on to say that Mr. Jacques was now 'in a very precarious state'.

Both the Reverend Joseph and his son Mervyn played cricket, and the Thicket Priory cricket team hosted numerous local sides at Thicket, winning more matches than they lost. Mervyn was a member of the York Cricket Club, for which his father paid 1 guinea annually for his membership. Thicket also had a football team, and 'The Priors' played football in the Derwent League. The priory also hosted several local angling groups to fish the Derwent from the priory grounds and many prize fish were caught there. The family was very active in the social scene of the Victorian period, attending many functions and charity events, and frequently organised fêtes at the priory for schools, workhouse children, and the elderly.

The Reverend's many pursuits, plus his charitable projects and his official duties in the county, meant that he could devote very little time to his local pastoral care. To remedy this situation he began a search for a curate to take on these duties at Thorganby church. Letters were sent out throughout 1864, and eventually a suitable candidate was found in the person of the Rev. Joseph Thomlinson.

With so many responsibilities on his shoulders time was of the essence to the Reverend. He even wrote a letter to the Secretary of the General Post Office in London complaining about the time that letters were normally delivered to Thicket Priory, generally about 10.30am, leaving him with no time to reply by the same post. He requested that the route for deliveries of letters in this area of the East Riding be rearranged so that he could he receive his letters earlier. It is not known if this request was granted.

The family was very well thought of in the area, due in no small part to the frequent charitable events held at Thicket – teas and outings for the orphans and schoolchildren of the locale, and the occasional generous gestures to their many tenants, such as was reported in the newspapers of March 1850:

> We have the pleasure of informing our readers that the Rev. J. D. Jefferson, of Thicket Priory, at his recent rent day, at the house of Mr. Bowman, the Commercial Inn, Howden, made a proposal to his numerous tenantry, either to return them ten per cent. on their half-year's rent, or allow them twenty per cent. in tillage.

The 1851 census tells us which family members were residing at Thicket Priory and also provides a snapshot of the household servants. The family included: Joseph Dunnington-Jefferson, head, 43, and is described as magistrate and perpetual curate at Thorganby; Anna Mervynia, wife, 38; and their children, Mervynia Jane,

10; Caroline Emma, 8; Mary Campbell, 6; Joseph John, 5; Theodosia, 2; and Mervyn, 1. The 12 servants were listed next, first the upstairs staff: Sarah Walmsley, 35, governess, of Tynemouth; Thomas Strickland, 31, footman, of Edstone, Yorks; Robert Gibbon, 25, coachman, of Whorlton, co. Durham; and John White, 16, page. The downstairs staff included: Elizabeth Balmborough, 58, housekeeper, of Yorkshire; Eliza Lascelles Cowburn, 42, nurse, of Bishopwearmouth; Jane Barton, 33, housemaid, of Acomb; Mary Kettlewell, 22, dairy maid, of Tadcaster; Mary Todd, 18, kitchen maid, of Askham Bryan; Ann Allison, 18, housemaid, of Thorganby; Anna Fletcher, 17, nursery maid, of York; and Mary Newsome, 61, labourer's wife, of Aughton. The other member of the family in the area, the Reverend Joseph's aunt, Jane Dunnington, 83, was living at nearby Thorganby Hall, accompanied by four servants: a cook and housemaid (combined); a dairy maid; a coachman; and errand boy. It is noticeable that there was no Thicket Lodge mentioned on the 1851 census, but it does appear from the census of 1861 onwards.

The Thicket Priory Estate was expanded again in 1858, when the Newbald Hall Estate was broken up and sold in lots at auction. The Reverend bought Bullens Hill Farm, of just over 254 acres for £12,700, and Sober-Hill Farm, of just over 477 acres for £19,000.

The 1861 census shows that the family had sadly lost a daughter, Caroline Emma, in the intervening ten years, but had gained a son, Thomas Trafford. Caroline Emma had died in a terrible accident at Scarborough as mentioned previously. Also on the census we learn that the servants were now supplemented by a lady's maid, a groom and an assistant laundry maid. Thicket Priory Lodge was now mentioned for the first time, where William Rogers resided with his wife and son, and where William, in addition to being the gatekeeper of Thicket Priory, was also employed as a gardener.

Thorganby Hall

Jane Dunnington was still going strong at Thorganby, and now aged 92, accompanied by her four servants.

Joseph is absent on the 1871 census, but his son Joseph John was there with his wife, Emma, showing she was aged 20, and had been born in Ireland. The house had a full complement of 10 servants, and Thicket Lodge was now occupied by William Smith and his family. Aunt Jane Dunnington of Thorganby Hall had died before this census year and was buried at Thorganby, 26 March 1863, and the hall was then leased to Charles Tunnard and his family.

The 1870s was to bring much joy to the Dunnington-Jefferson family, with two marriages to celebrate. First was of the eldest son, Joseph John, who married Emma Sarah Stoney, the second daughter of Mr. T. B. Stoney, JP, of Portland Park, Tipperary. The marriage took place in the village of Lorrah, Co. Down. The bridegroom was attended by the Count de Bros as his best man, with several army officers as groomsmen. The bride was attended by the three sisters of the groom, Mervynia, Mary Campbell and Theodosia, plus several other ladies. The ceremony was performed by the Venerable Archdeacon Knox, and afterwards a déjeuner was served to upwards of eighty guests under a marquee in Portland Park. After the celebrations the bride and groom left by special train for Dublin, en route to Wales.

Six years later it was the turn of Joseph John's sister to get married, Mary Campbell Dunnington-Jefferson. This was a less grand affair than that of the eldest son, and unusually did not take place in the home parish of the bride. The marriage ceremony was performed in the parish church of Saints Peter and Paul, Wadhurst, Sussex, where the groom, the Rev. Frederick Field-Richards, had previously been curate. He was now the English Chaplain at Toulon, the eldest son of Frederick Richards, The Briars, Hastings. They had one child, John Charles Field-Richards, who was a motorboat racing double gold medal winner in the 1908 Olympics. Mary's husband, Frederick, died in April 1879, and was buried in Hastings.

Back at Thicket, in the September of 1879, the lady of the house, Anna Mervynia, was advertising for a curate for Thorganby, to have sole charge and starting in the October, with a salary of £150 per annum, and to include a house. Her husband, the Rev. Joseph Dunnington-Jefferson was the perpetual curate at Thorganby, but was now in his seventies and possibly the curacy was getting too much for him.

The Reverend Joseph died 31 July 1880 and was buried a week later at Thorganby the following 6 August, aged 73. His obituary appeared in all the national and provincial newspapers of the day. The Reverend's youngest son, Thomas Trafford Dunnington-Jefferson, died the year after his father, at the relatively young age of 29, and was buried at Thorganby 4 April 1882.

The 1881 census reveals that at Thicket only one member of the family was in residence, Mervynia Jane, her age being given as 40 years, and her status as 'daughter of the head of household'. She was accompanied by nine servants: Sarah Steele, the cook and housekeeper; Emily Roxby, sewing maid; Mary Chaplin, housemaid; Anne Wallsington, laundry maid; Laura Hague, housemaid; Hannah Gibson, dairy maid; Sarah Smith, kitchen maid; George Ablet Hughes, footman; and Henry Davice, groom. Missing was the butler, who we know was Frederick Henry Babs in 1882.

The eldest son, Joseph John Dunnington-Jefferson, was educated at Eton and was admitted a pensioner at Trinity College, Cambridge in 1863, matriculating in 1864, and gaining his BA in 1868, and his MA in 1871. He was admitted into the Inner Temple in February 1868, and called to the bar in May 1871. He joined the Yorkshire Hussars, rising from sub-lieutenant to lieutenant in 1876 and to captain in 1883.

Joseph John was appointed deputy lieutenant of the East Riding of the County of York, and the Borough of Kingston-upon-Hull in February 1884, and selected as the Conservative Party candidate for the Morley Division in October 1885, and like his father, he was also a magistrate for the county.

In May 1885, the London newspapers were announcing the arrival of members of the aristocracy and gentry for the 'season', and included the entry: 'Mr. and Mrs. Dunnington-Jefferson have arrived at 4 Wilton Street, from Thicket Priory', indicating that they were very much into the Victorian societal scene at this time.

The second son of the Reverend Joseph, Mervyn Dunnington-Jefferson, was born on 10 February 1850, and baptised at Thorganby 31 March 1850. He was educated at Eton and joined the 33rd Regiment of Foot in 1869 as an ensign, rising to lieutenant in 1871. Initially serving at home, he saw his first overseas service in September 1869 when he was in the East Indies until April 1878, followed by service in the Cape of Good Hope until November 1879. The following year he was promoted to captain and again saw service in the East Indies 13 March 1880–12 March 1881, returning to his home depot 13 March 1881.

The captain then took a leave of absence to get married, on 5 May 1881, at St. Michael le Belfrey in York, to Louisa Dorothy Barry, the daughter of the late Reverend John Barry, rector of Great Smeaton. He retired from the army on half-pay 23 August 1881, and following a family tradition became a magistrate. Following his marriage, the captain and his wife led a somewhat peripatetic life. From at least March 1882 they were in the family's Wilton Street house in Belgravia, as their first child, Dorothy, was born there. However, in July 1882 they were living in the former home of the late John Grimston at Neswick Hall, near Driffield, and were still there as late as October 1884, though they visited Bournemouth in the April of 1884 where their son, John Alexander, was born.

In November 1886 the captain was living in Scarborough and in March 1889 the family was now living at Middlethorpe Hall near Bishopthorpe, to the south-east of York. The family was staying in Bath on the night of the 1891 census and only servants occupied Middlethorpe Hall. However the family was back at

Middlethorpe Hall for the 1901 census and was still at Middlethorpe in 1905, but before May 1906 they had moved into Thicket Priory. The captain and Louisa had six children, no two of which were born in the same place: daughters, Dorothy (born Wilton Street, Belgravia), Hilda (born 1 Jan 1887 in Scarborough) and Ella (born 23 May 1888 at Bishopthorpe); and sons, Mervyn (born 29 Mar 1883 at Neswick Hall, but died in infancy), John Alexander Dunnington-Jefferson, (born 10 Apr 1884 in Bournemouth), and Wilfrid Mervyn, (born 2 April 1892, at Middlethorpe Hall).

Middlethorpe Hall, now a hotel. (by: JThomas. Creative Commons Attribution-Share Alike 2.0 Generic)

The younger brother of the captain, Thomas Trafford Dunnington-Jefferson, was a barrister. He attended school in Cheam, Surrey before going up to Trinity, Cambridge, gaining a BA in 1875 then MA and LLM in 1878. He was admitted to the Inner Temple, 9 December 1874, and called to the bar 26 January 1878. Thomas died at the relatively young age of 29, 1 April 1882, at the Midland Hotel in London, but was taken back to his home parish and was buried at Thorganby. He died intestate, and administration of his estate, which amounted to just over £1,357, was granted to his brother, Joseph John Dunnington-Jefferson.

Joseph John Dunnington-Jefferson

When Joseph John and Emma were not at their Wilton Street town-house in Belgravia for the 'season' they would often entertain at Thicket Priory, which was usually reported in the newspapers of the day. Examples include a cover shoot in November 1885, where the guests included: 'Sir Henry and Lady Boynton, Mr. and Mrs. H. Bromley, Viscount Bangor, Colonel and Mrs. Henderson, Hon. P. Savile, Hon. Walter Maxwell, Misses Lettbridge, Hon. Martin Hawke, and Mr. Princep;' but it was not just the gentry and aristocracy that benefited from the largesse of the Dunnington-Jeffersons; in August 1887 they hosted a garden party where they entertained over 150 friends and neighbours from across the county. The party went on into the evening and the grounds of the priory were illuminated by large numbers of Chinese lanterns hung among the trees, and small coloured glass lamps were festooned across the lake, giving a fairy-like appearance. The evening culminated with a grand display of fireworks, and throughout music was provided by a band.

Hunting and shooting at Thicket Priory was strictly controlled by the gamekeepers, but fishing was allowed, and the many fishing clubs in the York area were regularly permitted to fish the waters of the Derwent from within the priory grounds.

Joseph John was, unsurprisingly, a dedicated Conservative, and a member of the York Conservative Association. Yearly excursions were arranged for members of the Association to Thicket Priory, and often attracted 150 members or more. The excursions were timed to coincide with the annual show and floral fête held by the cottagers of Thorganby, and East and West Cottingwith, while a band of the Yorkshire Hussars provided music. A cricket match was usually held between the Association and the priory, followed by a tea for all, altogether about four hours of pleasant entertainment. Many of those who attended were named in newspaper reports.

The closing years of the century were marked by three events. The first was a change in the law which equalised the death duties on real and personal property, the repercussions of which were only realised much later. The second was a fire that had broken out at Thicket Priory in May, 1897. The family was away at the time, probably in Wilton Street for the season, and only a few servants were at the house. The fire broke out in the housemaid's room, and the fire brigade was sent for and dispatched from York. Fortunately, by the time the engine had arrived at Thicket, the villagers had managed to extinguish the fire by means of buckets of water, but the housemaid's room was completely destroyed, including its furniture, and several windows had broken. It is not known if the housemaid kept her position! The second event was more melancholy, with the passing of Joseph John's mother, Anna Mervynia, 2 November 1898, at the good age of 86 years. Anna was buried at Thorganby, leaving a will.

The new century began with news of some of the inhabitants of Thorganby with connections to the priory. In the August of 1900 the funeral took place of the 'Oldest Inhabitant' of Thorganby. Mr. Thomas Barton was buried at Thorganby, and was described as 'the oldest inhabitant of the parish, having reached the age of 89. Years ago he was a farmer in the parish under the late Canon Jefferson. For more than forty years he has been employed at Thicket Priory.' And in April 1903 the sad news was announced that 'Mr. E. Carr, second keeper to Captain Jefferson, Thicket Priory, Cottingwith, has disappeared. The Derwent is being dragged.' The passing of another 'oldest tenant farmer' was reported in December 1907, when the death was announced, at the advanced age of 85 years, of Mr. George Holdridge, at North Duffield Lodge. He was described as a 'well-known and highly-respected East Riding agriculturalist', and 'one of the oldest tenant farmers on Captain Jefferson's Thicket Priory Estate, and had resided at North Duffield Lodge for over 44 years.' He was buried at Skipworth churchyard.

Returning to Thicket Priory and family affairs, July 1905 saw the start of Captain Jefferson's disposal of many of his outlying lands and cottages at Howden, Barmby on the Marsh, Bellasize, Eastrington and Bishopsoil. The sales were by auction, and totalled over 1,767 acres. The sale also included the historic Manor House in Howden, formerly the palace of the Bishops of Durham when they were lords of the manor. The sale of the Manor House alone fetched £2,550. It is unclear what prompted this disposal, as land was the mainstay of the gentry at this time. Did the captain need money? The auctioneers were Richardson and Pearce-Brown of Selby (this was Reginald Pearce-Brown, formerly the land agent and estate manager at Thicket Priory).

Also in 1905 saw news of the death of Mervynia Jane Dunnington-Jefferson, the sister of the captain and eldest daughter of Canon Joseph. She resided with her cousin at Langridge Rectory, but was brought home to be buried at Thorganby.

The next two items to be reported in the newspapers were curious and tragic. In December 1909 an advertisement appeared in the press:

> CHAUFFEUR-GARDENER desires situation, experienced workshop and private service driving, careful driver, clean licence; 5 years experience inside and outside gardening; references; total abstainer; present master going abroad. — Matthews, Thicket Priory, York.

The master of Thicket Priory was Joseph John, and there is no sign of him or his wife Emma (they had no children) in the 1911 census. Was this the 'present master going abroad'? So where had they gone? To stay with Emma's family back in Ireland perhaps? The only person in Thicket Priory in the 1911 census was a sole butler, Frederick Matthews. Was this the chauffeur in the 1909 advertisement above, or did the butler place the advertisement on behalf of the chauffeur?

Above and below, a Humber 16-24 with chauffeur, waiting outside Thicket Priory, c. 1910-1913

Tragic Event

Captain Mervyn was visiting his in-laws at the time of the 1911 census, but there was no sign of his wife, Louisa Dorothy. Was she abroad with her father-in-law? Certainly, things were not well with the captain, as the next piece of news was tragic and shocking.

On the evening of Wednesday, 21 March 1912, the captain was staying at the Royal Station Hotel in York, where he was engaged in conversation with two prominent York citizens, who reported that the captain appeared to be in his normal health, and afterwards seemed to be busily engaged in writing. Early the following morning he bought a first-class ticket and took the first 6.30am train to Hull. A fellow traveller on the train who knew the captain reported that the captain was restless and went to the window twice and eventually changed his compartment. The traveller reported that when he left the train at Nunburnholme the captain was still on the train.

What happened after that is something of a mystery. After passing Market Weighton station, but half a mile short of Kilingcotes station, the captain and the train parted company while the train was in full motion. It was not known at the time if he had jumped from the train, or fell accidently. He may have been stunned from an injury he sustained behind his ear as a result of his fall from the train.

Following an inquest it was revealed that the driver and fireman on another train, coming in the opposite direction to the captain's original journey, reported that the captain deliberately walked on the rails directly towards the oncoming train, despite it sounding its horn twice. The driver applied his brakes, but it was too late and the train ran over the unfortunate captain.

His injuries were horrific. The driver summoned assistance from Kiplingcotes Station and a communication was sent to the Market Weighton police. A policeman was then despatched who identified the body on the line as that of Captain Dunnington-Jefferson. His cheque book was found three quarters of a mile nearer Market Weighton, and £3 10s. in gold was found nearer the scene of the fatality. No writing was found on the body. The body of the captain was then removed to Market Weighton Station.

An inquest was held the following day when the jury heard from the witnesses, and returned a verdict that Captain Jefferson had 'committed suicide while in a state of unsound mind.'

The funeral of the captain was held on Monday, 26 March 1912, at Thorganby, the chief mourners being his widow, Louisa Dorothy, his second son Wilfrid Mervyn, his daughter Hilda, and his brother Joseph John. The immediate family were joined by Mr. John Warren Barry, Major Robert Mercer Barry, and the Rev. Henry T. Barry (brothers-in law), Mr. A Moscrop, Mr. and Mrs. Matthews, and Mrs. Humphries. His eldest son, Lieutenant John Alexander, could not attend, being with his regiment in India, nor could his two other daughters, Dorothy and Ella, but no reason was given.

A great many of the county gentry attended, including: Lord Deramore, Canon and Miss Grimston (Stillingfleet), Mr. A. R. Empson (Yokefleet Hall), Colonel Philip Saltmarshe, Mrs. Key (Fulford Hall).

Priory estate staff, tenant farmers, and many others also attended the funeral. A Mr. and Mrs. Edwin Gray of York were prevented from attending.

The children from Cottingwith school were ranged along the church path awaiting the arrival of the funeral party. Six of the estate servants acted as bearers, the coffin being carried on a bier.

Captain Dunnington-Jefferson left a will, dated 5 May 1906, while he was living at Thicket Priory. He bequeathed to his wife, using her second forename of Dorothy, 'all the plate, plated articles, furniture, linen, glass, china, pictures, prints, photographs, objects of virtu or curiosity, musical instruments, books, and other articles of household use or ornament which I brought from Middlethorpe Hall'.

He left all the rest of his personal estate, and all his real estate to his son, John Alexander. He appointed John Alexander and Wilfred Forbes Home Thomson of Nunthorpe executors of his will, and his wife to be the guardian of his infant children. The will was probated on 24 May 1912, at the Principal Probate Registry.

Thicket Priory III for Rent

The following year on 5 May 1913, the land agent, Andrew Moscrop, acting on behalf of Joseph John Dunnington-Jefferson, put Thicket Priory up for rent, 'with early entry'. It was described as having 5 reception rooms, billiard-room, 30 bed and dressing rooms, outside laundry, and stabling for 12.

Joseph John, now 67 years of age, and his wife, Emma, then led a quiet retirement, staying at their favourite haunts mainly in London and Bath. When Emma died in 1920 her address was given as 24 Bath Road, Reading, a fine old building, still standing today. She was then taken home and buried at Thorganby. When Joseph John died in 1928 his address was given as 60 Cumberland Road, Reading, but dying at Marloes Road, South Kensington, London W8.

The captain's widow, Louisa Dorothy, gave her residence as Ashcroft, Old Nunthorpe, York in 1915, in the obituary for her son, Lieutenant Wilfrid Mervyn Dunnington-Jefferson, killed during WWI. When Louisa Dorothy died in 1951, in her 99th year, her address at that time was given as 40 Cottesmore Court, London, W8. Louisa Dorothy was also buried at Thorganby.

CHAPTER 4
Estate Management

William Burland – Letter-Books – Reginald Pearce-Brown
Andrew Moscrop – James Eric Smith – Colin Bell

William Burland
Prior to the building of Thicket Priory in the 1840s, estate management was performed by solicitors or land agents on behalf of the estate owners and sometimes by the land owners themselves. They would collect the rents and renew or re-grant leases of the farms, cottages, tenements and land that comprised the estate. Shortly after the building of Thicket Priory in 1847 we hear for the first time of a local estate manager in connection with Thicket Priory, one William Burland. He first appears in the 1851 census returns, living in Thorganby Lodge and is described as 'Farm Bailiff'. In the 1861 and 1871 censuses he is still living in Thorganby and is now described as an 'Accountant', but now a James Petty also appears, described as 'Working Bailiff'. Their actual roles and responsibilities cannot be gleaned from census returns alone, but fortunately the letter-books of the Rev. Joseph Dunnington-Jefferson and his 'agent', William Burland, survive, and make for interesting reading.

Letter-Books
The letter-books containing letters emanating from the estate office are all from either the Reverend Joseph Dunnington-Jefferson or his estate manager, William Burland, but the letters from the Reverend are written in a variety of hands, suggesting that the Reverend wrote his letters, but before they were sent someone in the estate office copied the letters into the letter-books to keep a note of what had been written.

The letters are mixed, primarily concerning the estate, such as the purchasing of various goods and services, the hiring of staff, the collection of rents from tenants, etc., but they also contain the private letters of the Reverend Joseph.

The estate letters reveal that when it came to an application to acquire a farm tenancy, or an application for a household servant position, the Reverend Joseph always required references, which were all followed up by letters to the referees.

When it came to the tenancy of farms, these came directly to the estate office. Noticeably, the Reverend Joseph placed a high regard on the moral character of the applicant:

> 29 Feb 1864
> The Rev. A Clarke, of Elvington, York.
> *Concerning Mr. W Brown of Elvington who has applied to me for a farm at West Cottingwith of 120 acres. Request for opinion of him. Is he a moral man, has sufficient capital for such an undertaking, viz £500 or £600. Does he and his wife have your favourable opinion, are they church people? JDJ*

All applications for household servant positions came via the Register Office for Servants, Coney Street, York. A typical follow-up letter to a referee would read:

> 21 Apr 1865
> The Rev. J. E. Sampson.
> *Sir, John Grainger has offered himself to me as Footman. Opinion on him please, not his professional capabilities, but his moral character JDJ*

Occasionally the Reverend Joseph would be approached by a farm worker employed by one of his tenant farmers, hoping the Reverend could intervene in a grievance, which he sometimes did, as the next letter shows:

> 3 Apr 1865
> Mr. Henry Jackson, Escrick.
> *Sir, George Parker of Wheldrake has complained to me that you have refused to pay him wages for 3½ days amounting to 4s. 8d. Please settle with him. JDJ*

Incoming letters do not survive, only the outgoing letters in the letter-books, but sometimes the letter-books reveal the outcome of an application, as the next letter shows:

> 27 Apr 1865
> Mr Sysworth, Register Office for Servants, Coney Street, York.
> *I am sorry to say that the character I have received for John Grainger is not so satisfactory as I could have wished. I will venture, however, to engage him. His wages will be twenty two pounds a year. He may be at the White House, Coppergate, on Saturday at 3 o'clock. JDJ*

The letter-books occasionally contain Amalgamated Assessed Tax Returns, which contain the names of the household servants, the number of carriages and horses, the use of armorial bearings, the number of dogs, and the amount of tax or duty paid, such as this return in 1865:

Names of Servants 20/- Each	Capacity
Thomas Strickland	Butler
Richard Fowler	Footman
John Smillie	Coachman
George Keath	Groom
William Armitage	Groom
William Henry Roper	Gardener
James Crier	Gamekeeper
George Lancaster (duty 10/6)	Under Gamekeeper

Other Dutiable Items	Number
Carriages with four wheels, duty £3 10s. 0d.	3
Carriages less than four wheels 15s. 0d.	2

Dutiable Animals	Number
Horses exceeding 13 hands £1 1s. 0d. each	8
Horses exceeding 13 hands £0 10s. 6d. each	1
Ponies, £0 5s. 3d. each	0
Dogs	6

Other
Armorial Bearings, used by those chargeable the duty of £3 10s. 0d. for a four wheeled carriage - Yes

The letter-books end in 1870, and the estate manager, William Burland, Esq., died 30 April 1876 and was buried 5 May at Brotherton. No further letter-books survive, but they were almost certainly kept.

Reginald Pearce-Brown

From 1878 the Thicket Priory Estate was managed by Reginald Pearce-Brown, who lived at Thorganby Hall with his wife Edith, three sons and four servants. Reginald was an Oxford BA. He was responsible for forming the stud at Thicket of Hackneys and Shires in 1882/3, and also managed the Home Farm of over 1,000 acres. Reginald attended a great many of the agricultural shows, gaining prizes for the horses of Thicket. The 1881 census records Reginald as living at Thorganby Hall, where he is described as 'Land Agent', while James Petty, 'Farm Bailiff', is recorded at Thicket Farm House and Buildings. Reginald would often visit the stock sales in the area, particularly the stock sales of Messrs. Richardson at Selby, where Reginald would be described as 'agent to Mr. J. J. Dunnington-Jefferson, JP, Thorganby Hall.'

By 1889 the stud at Thicket was one of great renown. A typical report of the stud prior to a horse sale was recorded in one of the York newspapers for March of that year:

> *Mr. Jefferson has made plain his desire to improve the breed and usefulness of the horses in the possession of his own tenants and the farmers of the district. He has paid high prices for the best mares and stallions that could be obtained, and has, through his able and shrewd agent, Mr. R. Pearce-Brown, whose judgment has by results been proved to be almost faultless, secured animals which have produced progeny showing all the best characteristics of pure shire blood.*

The 1891 census recorded Reginald Pearce-Brown, land agent, once more residing at Thorganby Hall, but now there was a new farm bailiff, a John Bowson, residing at Thicket Farm.

In October 1892 it was time for pastures new and Reginald advertised in *The Field* magazine for another position in the country as an estate agent. The advertisement was apparently successful, as the following month a testimonial, accompanied by a cheque, was presented at Thorganby Hall, attended by a large circle of friends and tenants, but among the guest list Joseph John was noticeable by his absence.

Reginald had formed a partnership in 1893 with the proprietor of one of the livestock auctioneers, formerly known as Messrs. Richardson, of Selby, but with the passing of Mr. Richardson (the father), Mr. Richardson (the son) was also keen to form a new joint partnership. The new concern was now known as Richardson and Pearce-Brown, Auctioneers of Selby, and continued to sell and auction livestock from Thicket.

Pearce-Brown was immediatey replaced by Andrew Moscrop at Thorganby Hall, and sales of horses from the Thicket Stud were now handled by Andrew. The following year Andrew married Annie Chapman, daughter of the late Eccles Haigh of Liverpool.

Andrew Moscrop

The 1901 census records Andrew Moscrop of Thorganby Hall, land agent and auctioneer, and Edmund Gabbitas is now at Thicket Priory New Farm, as farm bailiff. As well as managing the Thicket Stud, Andrew was also responsible for acquiring additions to the estate. In August 1903, Moscrop attended an auction in Selby and purchased a parcel of land in East Cottingwith of just over three acres, on behalf of the Thicket Priory Estate, for £250; and in March 1905 he attended an auction in York where a small farm in East Cottingwith was one of the lots. The bidding started at £2,000 and was eventually knocked down to Mr. Moscrop for £3,580.

One of the unusual properties Mr. Moscrop was required to handle was Thicket Priory itself, when it was offered, furnished, with 3,500 acres of good mixed shooting, in April 1909. A pre-notice of availability 'next spring' had been advertised the previous December, possibly to coincide with the forthcoming 'season'. It does not appear that there were any takers.

All tenders for repairs and alterations to estate properties, including all outlying farms etc., needed to be submitted to Mr. Moscrop for his action. The estate office at Thorganby Hall would also provide plans, drawings and specifications for viewing by prospective tenderers. Occasionally, Mr. Moscrop acted as a judge at local agricultural shows, and he was an active member on the Yorkshire Agricultural Society Council.

Following the failure to find a tenant for Thicket Priory a different tack was tried in April 1916. Instead of the priory building being offered for rent, the grounds were offered instead, where shooting in over 3,500 acres, including 125 acres of coverts, were put up for rent.

Following World War I, Andrew Moscrop was awarded the OBE in the King's Birthday Honours, in June 1918, for services in connection with the war. He was described as 'a well known agriculturalist, a member of the Central Agricultural Wages Board, president of the York Board of Agriculture Advisory Committee on Food Production, a member of the Council of the Yorkshire Agricultural Society, secretary of the York Shorthorn Society, and a member of the Council of the Yorkshire Coach Horse Society, and a prominent figure in the agricultural world in the North.'

As well as these prestigious offices that Andrew Moscrop filled at Thorganby Hall, he was also responsible for the more mundane appointments of farm workers on the Thicket Priory Estate. In April 1920, for example, he advertised for a driver for a Fordson tractor, with a good cottage and garden as part of the remuneration, and in January 1925 he advertised for 'a strong Youth as an Assistant' on a pedigree pig farm.

Active to the end, Andrew Moscrop retired in 1933 and died 1 January 1936, aged 72, after a short illness. A widower by this time, and with no children, his passing was greatly mourned by all that knew him, and his death was recorded in all the Yorkshire newspapers of the day. He was buried 3 January 1936 at Thorganby, and the service was conducted by Canon Harrison, the Chancellor of York Minster.

Andrew Moscrop left an estate worth £9, 689, and his bequests included £500 to Dr. Bernardo's Homes, and £1 to each child on the register at West Cottingwith School. He also left £20 to his servant, Mary Lynn (if still serving), and £10 to all his other servants, both indoor and outdoor; £1,000 to Annie McNeil; and £500 each to Helen McNeil and Tom H. Dobson; and £250 to his cousin, Elizabeth Taylor. The residue was left to his sisters, Jane, Margaret and Edith, during their lives, and after to York County Hospital.

Thorganby House

James Eric Smith

Andrew Moscrop was succeeded by James Eric Smith who ran the estate office from 1933 to 1955, but out of Thorganby House, rather than Thorganby Hall. Thorganby House, a listed building, *circa* 1845, probably by Edward Blore, was occupied by the vicar of Thorganby from 1880–1926, and was located near the church and almost opposite the village hall.

Fortunately, the daughter of James Eric Smith, Eve Smith, was available for interview at the writing of this chapter, and was able to give a great deal of detail concerning the management of the estate by her father, the land agent.

> Q. How many direct employees did the estate office have?
> A. The the majority of the residents of Thorganby at that time were employed by the estate office, and included the bailiffs, gamekeepers, joiner, blacksmith and several others. In addition there were tractor drivers and ploughmen and other agricultural workers who worked the two farms directly under the estate, Thicket Home Farm and Thorganby Home Farm. There were only a handful of incomers to the village.

Q. Where did your father come from?
A. My father came from Northumberland and prior to Thicket he worked on the Middleton Hall Estate. Although not a qualified veterinary he took a keen interest in animal welfare and was able to administer animal first aid when the need arose.

Q. Did your father work alone in the estate office?
A. On taking up his position at the Thicket Priory Estate office my father took on a secretary, Frances Hyndsley, who proved invaluable.

Q. Where was the estate office located?
A. It was inside Thorganby House in a room on the right of the entrance hall.

Q. Did Thorganby House have any servants?
A. We had one full-time maid, a Frances Hardcastle, plus two ladies who came from the village daily to do cleaning work, plus a Lizzy Knot who came to do the laundry and ironing. Outside, there was a groom who looked after father's horse and the Shetland ponies which myself and my brother rode. The house had no cook, as mother liked to do her own cooking. Mother was a teacher by profession, and while at Thorganby House she started the local Women's Institute.

Q. Tell me about the house.
A. The house was large, with cellars used for storing apples, but I think it was a wine cellar previously. The cellar would often flood, up to a depth of two to three feet. On the ground floor was the estate office, drawing room, dining room, kitchen and scullery. The upper floor had around twelve rooms, ten of which served as bedrooms, and at times we shared the house with the local vicar and his family. During WWII we also hosted two young evacuees from Hull, Dick and Harry.

Q. What technical facilities did the estate office have?
A. It had a telephone. [At least by 27 April 1945, as at that date Mr. Smith advertised in the local newspapers for the return of a lost polled heifer, and asked to be informed at the estate office on Telephone: Wheldrake 13]. *There was no grid electricity to the house in 1953, but electrical power was supplied by an outside generator located in an outbuilding.*

Thank you very much, Eve.

Mr. Smith continued to advertise for workers in the early 1950s. Even for general farm hands the estate office would often specify that the man should apply with references and be married. In return the estate offered a good three-bedroomed cottage in the village as part of the terms of employment.

Mr. Smith, like his predecessors, also combined estate work with agricultural offices in the county and was a member of local committees. He was the Yorkshire branch secretary of the County Landowners Association from at least May 1950, and chairman of the Thorganby Church Restoration Committee. He also acted as land agent for other Yorkshire estates.

The last advertisement available from the British Newspaper Archive concerning the Thicket Priory Estate appeared on 29 October 1955, when Mr. Smith advertised for a 'general farm worker' offering a good house with mains water, near a school, and for '2 young single men' to live in, as second tractor driver and general farm worker.

Colin Bell

The estate office under Mr. Smith continued until 1964, when the family moved on following the sale of the Thicket Priory Estate by Sir John Dunnington-Jefferson, Bt. to Mr. John Bealby Eastwood in that year, though Mr. Smith continued to advise Mr. Eastwood's new estate manager, Colin Bell, right up to his (Mr. Smith's) death in 1976.

John Bealby Eastwood was born 9 January 1909 and attended the Queen Elizabeth Grammar School in Mansfield. He was knighted in July 1975 and was made a CBE in 1980. He made his fortune in the integrated chicken and egg market and became one of the largest producers in the world. He sold the Thicket Priory Estate for around £4 million in 1978 and died in Farnsfield, Nottinghamshire, 6 August 1995.

The Thicket Priory Estate was purchased from Sir John Bealby by Humberts, the property agents, on behalf of the British Gas Corporation Pension Fund, and they installed their own estate manager, Andrew Mason, who resided at Thorganby Hall. Over the subsequent years the houses were sold to the tenants by British Gas and the estate is now all but extinguished.

CHAPTER 5
WWI and the Inter-War Years

John Alexander Dunnington-Jefferson – Wilfrid Mervyn Dunnington-Jefferson
Ella Dunnington-Jefferson – WWI Roll of Honour – The Inter-War Years

John Alexander Dunnington-Jefferson

John (Jack to his friends) Alexander Dunnington-Jefferson, the elder son of Captain Mervyn Dunnington-Jefferson and his wife, Louisa Dorothy, was educated at Eton and attended Sandhurst, joining the 3rd Battalion Royal Fusiliers (City of London Regiment) in 1904 becoming a 2nd Lieutenant 2 March 1904 and Lieutenant 9 December 1905.

He served initially in the Bermuda Garrison during the early part of 1905 but departed Bermuda for Cape Town, South Africa, aboard the HMT (His/Her Majesty's Transport, in other words a troopship) *Soudan* on 18 December 1905. Serving in South Africa for several years the battalion moved to Mauritius, which is where he was enumerated in the 1911 census, but later that year he and the 3rd moved again, this time to Lucknow in India, which prevented him from attending his father's funeral in March 1912.

With the onset of WWI the 3rd departed Lucknow arriving in England in December of that year. John Dunnington-Jefferson had been promoted to captain 4 September 1912 and joined the newly formed Intelligence Corps section of the Headquarters Staff as a temporary major and was graded for purposes of pay as a General Staff Officer, 2nd Grade. Major J. A. Dunnington-Jefferson RF replaced Captain, later Field Marshal Lord Wavell as the Corps Commandant from December 1914 to February 1916 and was responsible for establishing the high reputation of the Corps during WWI.

On the war memorial in Holborn to The Royal Fusiliers (City of London Regiment), erected in 1922, there is one line of inscription which reads: 10TH (B) – – (INTELLIGENCE CORPS). The 'B' branch of the Intelligence Corps was the Security Duties Section, responsible for security behind the lines and in which Major Dunnington-Jefferson served.

During the war, Major Dunnington-Jefferson earned the Distinguished Service Order (DSO) in 1917 and was mentioned in despatches (MiD) six times; among other awards he received the French Legion of Honour, the Belgian War Cross and the Italian Order of St. Maurice and St. Lazarus. He ended the war a brevet major and retired from the army in 1919 as a lieutenant colonel.

Wilfrid Mervyn Dunnington-Jefferson

Jack's younger brother, Wilfrid Mervyn, did not fare so well. Educated at Radley College, Wilfrid went up to Christ Church, Oxford in 1910 and was reading for the bar at the Inner Temple when he volunteered at the outbreak of the war in 1914. He enlisted with the rank of 2nd Lieutenant in the 7th Battalion, Royal Fusiliers and went to the front in Belgium in April 1915 attached to the 3rd Battalion, his elder brother's battalion. Wilfrid was killed in action near Gravenstafel in the Second Battle of Ypres, 25 April 1915.

Various dates have been given for Wilfrid's death. However, following information in a letter dated 8 May (1915) from Jack Dunnington-Jefferson to his mother and provided by Wilfrid's niece, Nicky Dunnington-Jefferson, this quote has come to light which surely verifies Wilfrid's date of death.

> *I went out to see the 3rd Bn. yesterday. Wilfrid was killed on the 25th April at a place called Gravenstafel, just North of Zonnebeke, near Ypres. He was buried where he fell, as it was impossible to bring away any of our officers.*

2nd Lieutenant Wilfrid Mervyn Dunnington-Jefferson's address at death was given as Ashcroft, Old Nunthorpe, York.

Ella Dunnington-Jefferson

It was not just the menfolk of the Dunnington-Jefferson family that were involved in the war effort. A sister of John Alexander and Wilfrid Mervyn, Ella Dunnington-Jefferson, was also involved.

Ella served first as a nurse and orderly at Clifford Street and Nunthorpe Hall Auxiliary Hospitals. These Voluntary Aid Detachment (VAD) hospitals were convalescent hospitals for injured and traumatised military personnel, and she must have seen much suffering. Ella then moved to T. E. Cooke's, when it opened in 1915 at Bishophill in York. This company specialised in making scientific instruments and equipment for the military, including rangefinders and surveying equipment and when they opened they took on many women to help with production. While working at Cooke's, Ella wrote a poem describing life at the instrument factory.

A Munition Dirge

I was a nurse, a nurse was I,
Methought at Cooke's I'll have a try

The rain poured down, the wind blew shrill,
O'er "Cookes-s;ss" Works on Bishophill.

I knocked upon the factory door,
I stood upon the office floor.

The manager spoke unto me:
"Munitions worker you would be"?

Quoth I, "I am a V.A.D.
But if you're kind I'll work for thee."

Quoth he — "It is a stiffish job,
You'll have to come for 17/- Bob".

"Be here quite sharp at early dawn,
And unto secrecy be sworn."

"At Bishophill you'll stay until
You faint before the awful drill."

They led me from the fated room
Into a dungeon full of gloom.

I sat upon a wooden stool,
I vowed I was an awful fool.

I painted reel, I painted drum,
I cut my hand, I pierced my thumb.

I drove the nail, I turned the screw
I did what'eer there was to do.

But when I saw the ladies there,
My heart leaped up, they were so fair.

Miss Tennant took me by the hand,
"Oh welcome to Munition Land".

"I'll give you buns, I'll give you tea,
And Chocolate Biscuits I'll give thee".

And dear Miss Carr, she said to me:
"We're only here on suffrance see".

Miss Blaylock works what'eer may hap,
She swallowed strip, she swallowed flap.

Her sister sat beside her too,
I gave here all my work to do.

Miss Turner left her home, her cats,
To work upon the old green felt mats.

Miss Dodsworth came from far-off France,
To drive the nail, discard the lance.

Her sister came from Nunthorpe, See!!
She also was a V.A.D.

And Mrs Hearder came from far,
To show what women workers are.

Miss Radcliffe sat among the paint.
And gazed on Eastern gardens quaint.

Miss Bury painted like a dear,
But on her work shed many a tear.

There was Harrison, our Overseer,
Who caused us all to quake with fear.

Oh Harri - son, Oh Harri - son,
A dreadful work you've started on.

I once did to the palace start,
With white kid gloves and quaking heart.

Where Mrs Leetham worked apace,
With Mrs Rudgard in a race.

Miss Moxon sat in queenly state,
With love of work, inborn, innate.

Miss Wright — who came from Harro-gate.
And turned up ne'er a moment late.

The Bubble-people sit below,
And bubbles all day long they blow.

Within the glass-shop, good and staid,
The skilled workers ply their trade.

And when you're feeling very low,
Oh! Come to Cooke's, Heigho!! Heigho!!

Miss Tennant dear, will give you tea,
You'll be in splendid companee.

Mid'st shower and rain in far-off Lands,
Our soldiers fight with eager hands.

We cannot join their splendid throng.
Drive back the foe, make right the wrong.

To drive the nail, to turn the screw,
Is what we women all can do.

And even, when the work is slow,
Are we at Cooke's downhearted? No!!

E. D. Jefferson

A Munition Dirge survives today in the archived records of Cooke's at the Borthwick Institute for Archives at York University.

WWI Roll of Honour

The men of the parish suffered a number of losses during WWI, and the names of the men who lost their lives in what became known as the Great War have been memorialised on a plaque in St. Helen's Church, Thorganby.

TO THE GLORY OF GOD AND IN MEMORY OF THE
MEN OF THIS PARISH WHO GAVE THEIR LIVES
IN THE SERVICE OF THEIR COUNTRY DURING
THE GREAT WAR 1914–1919.

WILFRID MERVYN DUNNINGTON JEFFERSON, R. FUS., KILLED IN ACTION APRIL 25TH, 1915.
HERBERT HANLEY, COLDSTREAM GUARDS, KILLED IN ACTION SEPT. 15TH, 1916.
ARCHIE SPENCER, COLDSTREAM GUARDS, KILLED IN ACTION SEPT. 15TH, 1916.
GEORGE HENRY WILSON, ROYAL ARMY MEDICAL CORPS, KILLED IN ACTION AUGUST 19TH, 1916.
JOHN HENRY LANCASTER, WEST YORKS REGT., DIED SEPT. 12TH, 1917.
LEONARD CLAUDE GOSLEY, COLDSTREAM GDS., KILLED IN ACTION DECEMBER 5TH, 1917.
FRED DITCHBURN, ROYAL FIELD ARTILLERY, DIED JANUARY 26TH, 1918.
WILLIAM JAMES MOFFAT, ROYAL SCOTS GREYS, KILLED IN ACTION MARCH 23RD, 1918.
ARTHUR WILSON, HAMPSHIRE REGT., KILLED IN ACTION SEPTEMBER 1ST, 1918.
ARTHUR IBBOTSON THOMPSON, KING'S OWN YORKS LT. INF., DIED MAY 24TH, 1919.
NORMAN GILL COSSINS, LONDON REGT., DIED OF WOUNDS WHILE A PRISONER OF WAR.

"MAKE THEM TO BE NUMBERED WITH THY SAINTS
IN GLORY EVERLASTING."

Further details on the above men are as follows:

Herbert Hanley of Thorganby, Yorks, Private Coldstream Guards, Reg. No. 14506, enlisted in Newark, fought in France and Flanders, killed in action 16 September 1916.

Archie Spencer of Thorganby, Yorks, Private Coldstream Guards, Reg. No. 15542, enlisted in Pocklington, fought in France and Flanders, killed in action 15 September 1916.

George Henry Wilson of Hull, Yorks, Gunner Royal Horse Artillery and Royal Field Artillery, Reg. No. 75618, enlisted in Hull, fought in France and Flanders, killed in action 1 November 1914.

Leonard Claude Gosley, born Goodmanham, resided at Market Weighton, Yorks, Private Coldstream Guards, Reg. No. 15896, enlisted in Hull, transferred as a Guardsman to the 4th Battalion, Guards Machine Gun Regiment, Reg. No. 529, fought in France and Flanders, killed in action 16 September 1916.

Fred Ditchburn of York, Bombadier Royal Horse Artillery and Royal Field Artillery, Reg. No. 45039, enlisted in York, fought in Salonika, killed in action 26 January 1918.

William James Moffat of Hawick, Roxburgh, Corporal Household Cavalry and Cavalry of the Line (incl. Yeomanry and Imperial Camel Corps), 2nd Dragoons Battalion, (Scots Greys), fought in France and Flanders, killed in action 23 March 1918.

Arthur Wilson born West Cottingwith, residing at Howdendyke, Yorks, Private Hampshire Regiment, 10th Battalion, Reg. No. 16750, enlisted in Hull, fought in Balkans, killed in action 1 September 1918.

Arthur Ibbotson Thompson. Also commemorated on a memorial in Rawmarsh, and on a headstone in Thorganby churchyard. Husband of Emily Mary Thompson, of 13, Aldwarke Rd., Parkgate, Rotherham. Private King's Own Yorkshire Light Infantry. His service record lists that he served in Germany from 18 November 1916 to 26 December 1917 and in Switzerland from 27 December 1917 until 13 June 1918. Captured near Cambrai on 18 November 1916. Recorded as POW at Limburg, Hesse on 17 April 1917, at

Worms, Hesse on 23 July 1917 and Weiler (?) on 25 February 1918. On his return home in June 1918 he was assessed for future service and was discharged as unfit in July 1918, suffering from TB contracted during his period as a POW.

Norman Gill Cossins, born Topcliffe, residing at Thorganby, Yorks, Private Royal Fusiliers (City of London Regiment) 3rd Battalion, Reg. No. 67621, enlisted in Selby, fought in France and Flanders, but was sadly killed in action 26 October 1917.

The Inter-War Years

Following the end of WWI and his retirement from his regiment, Lieutenant Colonel John Alexander Dunnington-Jefferson returned to his home in Thicket Priory to pursue public service in local county affairs. First on his agenda, however, was to get the Thicket Priory Estate back into shape. During the war years there had been a dearth of available workers both inside and outside of the priory despite many advertisements, and the situation immediately after the war had not improved. Perhaps a shortage of tenant farmers also led to the colonel putting five freehold farms belonging to the estate up for sale in September 1919. Only one was sold, Northfield House Farm with 148 acres of land, the incumbent tenant, Thomas Watson, junior, selling for £3,000.

Less than two years later the colonel and his uncle, Joseph John, decided to disentail Thicket Priory and convert it to a fee simple, which was usually done if the intent was to eventually sell the property.

Some semblance of normality did start to appear in the 1920s. The Thicket Priory football team, The Priors, were back in action, playing away at Barmby Moor, but they were two men short due to harvesting and substitutes had to be found. Unfortunately, there was some sad news in March 1928, when the colonel's uncle, Joseph John Dunnington-Jefferson, died. At the time of his death his residence was given as 28 Marloes Road, South Kensington, London W.8. Joseph John was brought home to Thicket and was buried at Thorganby, 26 March 1928, aged 82.

The colonel also made some changes at Thicket Priory itself. He leased the priory for a five-year term to another colonel and his family, Lieutenant Colonel C. G. Maude and his wife in 1928, and they had a son born in 1926 while living at the priory. In 1930 another family occurs, giving their address as Thicket Priory, when Mr. John Wingfield Ford, the only son of Mr. and Mrs. Edward Vyvyan Ford, of Thicket Priory, was married to Miss Vera Hall Chalker, only daughter of Mr. and Mrs. Henry Chalker of Medindie, Sandal.

The early 1930s were marked by two unfortunate events. In August 1930 the York Fire Brigade had to be called out again, but this time at Home Farm, Thicket Priory, when the brigade had to work for 10 hours to put out a fire at a Dutch barn of eight sections full of the season's hay; and in September 1831 a verdict of 'accidently drowned' was returned at an inquest into the death of little John Hearn, the son of the head gardener at Thicket, who drowned in the Derwent while fishing with his playmates.

On the estate side of things Thicket was still having problems finding tenants for its farms. Lawns House Farm at North Duffield was advertised in September 1930, then again in February 1932 and September 1932, while an advertisement in August 1932 offered 'Some Farms of handy sizes' to be let from Lady Day 1933, and another offered Woodfield Farm of 45 acres of grass and 199 acres of arable, also in the advertisement of September 1932.

Lawns House Farm was offered yet again in January 1934 along with Thorganby Hall Farm, which itself was offered again in September 1934. Clearly, finding and retaining tenant farmers was certainly an onerous task for the estate manager, Andrew Moscrop, in the inter-war years.

The mid-1930s saw two more deaths. In November 1935 Mr. Arthur Thomas Farr, aged 69, a joiner on the estate, was found dead in the estate workshop, having been employed on the estate for 53 years; and in January 1936 Andrew Moscrop, Esq., the estate manager and land agent also died. He was a widower and had no children; his passing was a great loss to the estate and to the many organisations of which he was a member. He was 72.

Andrew Moscrop was succeeded as estate manager by James Eric Smith, but he managed the estate out of Thorganby House rather than Thorganby Hall, as has been stated earlier. Mr. Smith was always known as Jim Smith.

Some significant events in the life of Colonel Dunnington-Jefferson also occurred over the same period. When the lease to Colonel Maude of the priory expired in 1933 the building was unoccupied for more than five years, and was unoccupied in *The 1939 Register*, a sad state of affairs.

In December 1936, Colonel Dunnington-Jefferson was appointed as the new Deputy Lord Lieutenant of the East Riding of Yorkshire. In reporting this, the *Hull Daily Mail* gave a brief biography of the Colonel:

> *Lieutenant-Colonel Dunnington-Jefferson, whose home is Thicket Priory, York, was elected chairman of the East Riding County Council on May 1 last in succession to the late Lord Deramore, defeating Alderman T. D. Fenby by a majority vote.*
>
> *The new Deputy Lieutenant is 53 years of age and is a bachelor. He was educated at Eton and then went to Sandhurst. He joined the Royal Fusiliers in 1904 and after a distinguished military career retired in 1919. He served throughout the European war and was six times mentioned in despatches, his decorations including St. Maurice and St. Lazarus (Italy), Couronne and Croix de Guerre (Belgium) and Legion of Honour (France), together with the D.S.O.*
>
> ### INTEREST IN AGRICULTURE
> *Lieutenant-Colonel Dunnington-Jefferson has done a great work for agriculture, notably in connection with the Great Yorkshire Show, much of the success of which, this year at Beverley, was due to his enthusiasm and energy as hon. director. He is a member of the Yorkshire Agricultural Society, and has done a great deal to encourage modern developments in farming. He is a vice-chairman of the Yorkshire Council for Agricultural Education, and has been keenly interested the new Agricultural Institute for Yorkshire at Askham Bryan.*
>
> *He has been an active member of the East Riding County Council for 14 years, and it has been said of him: "There is no one with a higher sense of public duty."*
>
> *He himself is a landowner, and is well known as a breeder of cattle and sheep. He is a director of the Yorkshire Insurance Company and a trustee of the York County Savings Bank.*
>
> *A keen sportsman, he is chairman of the Hunt Committee of the York and Ainsty Hunt. He is a member of the Yorkshire Club, York.*

The biggest events, however, were still to come in 1938, and also made clear who was now living at Thorganby Hall:

> **Lieut.-Colonel to Wed**
> The engagement is announced between Lieut.-Col. J. A. Dunnington-Jefferson, D.S.O., eldest son of the late Captain M. Dunnington-Jefferson of Thicket Priory, York, and Mrs. Dunnington-Jefferson, 40 Cottesmore Court, London, W.8, and Isobel, daughter of Lieut.-Col. H. A. Cape, D.S.O. of Thorganby Hall, York.
>
> **Thorganby Wedding: Colonel Dunnington-Jefferson and Miss Isobel Cape**
> The marriage of Lieut-Colonel J. A. Dunnington-Jefferson and Miss Isobel Cape, younger daughter of Lieut.-Colonel H. A. Cape, and the late Mrs Cape, of Thorganby Hall, took place very quietly on Saturday at Thorganby.
>
> Owing to the critical situation earlier in the week, arrangements previously made for the wedding to take place in London were cancelled. Only relatives, personal friends and tenants and employees on the Thicket Priory Estate were present.

The 'critical situation' referred to was the ongoing meeting between Prime Minister Neville Chamberlain and German Chancellor Adolf Hitler in Berchtesgaden in an attempt to negotiate an end to German expansionist policies, and the warning that England and France gave to Czechoslovak President Edvard Beneš to tell him Britain and France would not fight Hitler if he decided to annex the Sudetenland by force. While at home, Winston Churchill warned of grave consequences to European security if Czechoslovakia was partitioned.

War seemingly had been averted when Chamberlain signed the Munich Agreement with Hitler, and returned to the UK on 30 September waving the Agreement and giving the now infamous speech in Downing Street, declaring 'Peace in our Time'.

It was all an illusion.

CHAPTER 6

WWII and the Post-War Years

Lieutenant Colonel Sir John Alexander Dunnington-Jefferson
Remembrances – Social Changes – The Return of the Nuns
Subsequent Ownership and Thicket Priory IV

Lieutenant Colonel Sir John Alexander Dunnington-Jefferson

The United Kingdom declared war on Germany on 1 September 1939 following Germany's invasion of Poland in full breach of their commitments in the Munich Agreement.

In 1939 there was only one male in the Dunnington-Jefferson family, Lieutenant Colonel John Alexander Dunnington-Jefferson, but he had retired from the army back in 1919 and was ineligible for call-up, but that did not stop him from taking on several civilian roles to support the war effort.

The colonel, who was Chairman of the East Riding County Council, was further appointed as the Chairman of the East Riding War Agricultural Executive Committee, which had its headquarters in St. Mary's Manor in Beverley and was composed of several departments: Cultivation Department, which was mainly concerned with seeing that all land was properly cultivated, with eight district officers, who went round and knew the area and made recommendations about the cultivation orders; the Milk Department, whose job was to see that as much milk was produced from the cows as possible; the Livestock Department, whose remit was to improve the quality of livestock; the Labour Department who had the supervision of POWs (mainly Italian, but some German POWs also) and the Land Army girls, finding them accommodation and directing them to various places; and the Demonstrations Department, whose function was to introduce the most modern and up-to-date farming techniques and new machinery to the farmers of the East Riding. Farmers who did not follow the directives of the committee by failing to maximise output from their land under cultivation could be, and were, ejected from their farms and replaced. One farmer, a Mr. Mason, was ejected from his farm in Birdsall for failing to manure his land properly, and his tenancy terminated. The committee certainly took their goals seriously.

The estate management continued as normal during the war years, attempting to find new tenants for the estate's farms, such as Thorganby Hall Farm and Ings View Farm, both in April 1940.

At family level, the colonel was bereaved of his great-aunt, Theodosia Dunnington-Jefferson, who died at the grand age of 92 in London. She had not lived in the Thicket Priory area for many years following the death of her father, the Rev. Joseph Dunnington-Jefferson. Theodosia left an estate valued at £8,255 and bequeathed £50 to Peter the cat and Billy the dog. She made several other charitable bequests and some poignant bequests to the staff of the hotel where she had been living, stating, 'I wish to thank them for the great humane kindness that they have always shown to me and made a lonely soul happier.'

In 1941, on 12 February, Jack Dunnington-Jefferson and his wife, Isobel, were to celebrate the birth of their first child, a daughter, Rosemary Nicolette. Their second child, a son, Mervyn Stewart, was born 5 August 1943.

At priory staff level, the colonel began to advertise for a chauffeur in June 1941 for his daily commute to Beverley and occasional trips to York and other places where his duties took him. The applicant needed to be over military age, or exempt from service, and a cottage would be provided. The post was advertised again in August 1941.

In December 1942 the colonel was to be promoted yet again, when his role of Deputy Lieutenant of the East Riding of Yorkshire was made up to vice-lieutenant to act in the absence of the Lieutenant of the County, Colonel Michael Guy Percival Willoughby, 11th Baron Middleton, who commanded the 5th and 30th Battalions of the East Yorkshire Regiment during WWII.

Returning to the war effort, the labour shortage on farms had become extremely acute by May of 1941 so the colonel, as Chairman of the East Riding War Agricultural Executive Committee, placed advertisements in the Yorkshire newpapers advising farmers who were short of labour to employ the ladies of the Women's Land Army (WLA). The take-up of the ladies of the WLA was slow, and resisted by some farmers, so the colonel appealed again in the March of 1942, reminding farmers that there were no reserves whatever of skilled men and that alternative forms of unskilled labour must now be sought, and directed them once more to the WLA.

The war effort did, however, provide new opportunities for skilled but dying trades. The village blacksmith, whose skills were becoming less and less in demand with only the occasional horse to shoe owing to the wholesale replacement of horses by the motor car and tractor, was given a lifeline by the war. Vehicles and farm machinery of all sorts were employed in the war effort and when, for example, a cog lost a tooth it was a costly and time-consuming exercise to get the cog replaced. Some forward thinking brains in the Ministry of Agriculture had the idea to retrain the village blacksmiths in welding techniques, not a huge jump from the traditional blacksmith skills, but it meant that cogs and other mechanical parts could now be repaired on the spot rather than waiting for replacement parts. George Simpson, Thorganby's blacksmith, was one such smith that benefited from this retraining and became an important war worker. He obtained his proficiency certificate in oxyacetylene welding and could then repair tractors and any other type of farm machinery, raising his status and demand considerably in the locality. George's son, Geoffrey, a 16-year-old lad, had already spent two years at technical college and now joined his father in tractor classes, while George found time to give lectures to other craftsmen of the benefits of retraining.

It would appear that the earlier pleas to farmers in 1941 and 1942 to utilise the labour provided by the WLA had borne fruit, and there was now a large contingent of WLA girls in the county, under the direction of the East Riding Committee, the chairman of which was the colonel's wife, Frances Isobel Dunnington-Jefferson, who was also made a Justice of the Peace in December, 1944.

Sir John Alexander Dunnington-Jefferson

In June 1944 the king approved the knighthood of Lieutenant Colonel John Alexander Dunnington-Jefferson which was formally announced 18 July 1944, and gazetted in *The London Gazette* 21 July 1944, p. 3146.

Following Victory in Europe, on 8 May 1945, it was time to honour the efforts of the East Riding agricultural workers in the war effort.

Lieutenant Colonel Dunnington-Jefferson had already been rewarded with a knighthood, but the girls of the WLA also received recognition, via Armlets, with Winifred Preston, c/o Mrs. Hesslewood of Thicket Priory Lodge being one such recipient.

Unfortunately, there is no memorial to the fallen of WWII in Thorganby or any list of those who served.

This may be due to censorship at the time.

Remembrances
Mention has been made earlier of the birth of Sir John's children, Rosemary Nicolette (Nicky) and Mervyn Stewart (died 9 January 2014). As at the writing of this book Nicky is the last remaining Dunnington-Jefferson former resident of Thicket Priory, and I was lucky enough to interview Nicky in September 2020 concerning her remembrances of Thicket.

Q. Do you remember the servants at Thicket?
A. Oh yes! There was Schofield, the butler; Miss Dawson, the cook; Louis, the housekeeper; and Elizabeth, Helen, Lucy and Jean, the maids, but perhaps they weren't all there at the same time; and MacFarlane, the chauffeur. I remember 'Mac' better than anyone. He taught me to drive.

Q. Was the family still riding while you were there?
A. Well, my father still had his hunter, Crosshands, nicknamed Ponto. I know this because I was told that Ponto was the first horse I ever 'rode', aged three! Merv and I had ponies, but we learnt to ride on a donkey called Neddy. I think my father gave up riding and sold his hunters when I was very small as I don't remember horses in the park at Thicket until our ponies came along.

Q. Did your mother not ride?
A. Oh, good God, no! She was terrified of horses! She did help with rounding up the ponies though when we wanted to ride, which was almost every day, as we both loved it. My maternal grandfather, Colonel Cape, who was living at Thorganby Hall at the time, taught us both to ride. He had been a cavalry officer so we couldn't have had a better instructor.

Q. So, presumably you had a stable-lad, or groom?
A. No. Merv and I had to take care of the ponies ourselves: feed them, rub them down after riding, groom them, clean the tack and muck out the stables...everything. And our mother saw to it that we didn't shirk our duties. I know however that my father had a groom, Allison, when he had hunters, before we came along.

Q. Did you ever fish, being so close to the river?
A. No, not proper fishing but we used to go down to the river (Derwent) to catch tiddlers in a net. The lake did have fish in it though, mainly pike, and there were also eels. But we certainly collected tadpoles and tried to hatch them into frogs! And we were fascinated by the toads too which were in the garden and under logs in the woods.

Q. What do you remember about the layout of Thicket Priory, and how many bedrooms did it have?
A. I remember the wooden staircase on the left in the entrance hall and there were big tapestries on the walls up the stairs. The morning room with my father's desk was the last room on the right at the end of the flagstoned hall and next to it was the library where we had a table tennis table. There was another big room immediately on the right after you came up the stone steps into the hall but it was seldom used. The dining room was past the staircase and down a passage to the left and the room was on the right. I am not sure how many bedrooms there were because we weren't allowed into the servants' quarters. And we weren't allowd to go up the tower either which was very annoying.
Also, I never remember the chapel being open. Basically the family occupied four bedrooms. My mother and father had their bedrooms and my brother and I each had a bedroom. There was a fifth bedroom up on the landing for guests and also a room for our nanny. And I also remember the schoolroom, near my mother's bedroom, as my brother and I had a governess, Miss Caldwell...we called her 'Mickey'. When I think back to my early childhood I realise how fortunate we were to be brought up in such lovely surroundings in the country. I remain a country lass at heart, with an inborn love of Yorkshiren and it is Thicket I really think of as 'home', even after all these years and the inevitable changes of ownership.

Q. What do you remember about the gardens at Thicket Priory?
A. I remember the gardens very well indeed; they were beautiful and very well kept. I particularly remember the glorious daffodils over on the other side of the lake, and the sweet scent of the primroses that grew among the rocks. Come to think of it, the rocks

were probably part of the remains of a former priory. As children, my brother and I sold posies of primroses to visitors when we opened the gardens.

And there was a special garden next to the kitchen garden where my mother would pick most of the flowers (dahlias, lupins, sweet William, Michaelmas daisies, nasturtiums etc.) that she always arranged in the house. Thicket was always full of sweet-smelling blooms. She loved flowers and her favourites were lily of the valley and sweet peas. In the kitchen garden I remember especially the smell of the small box hedges…whenever I smell box, I think of Thicket. Also, my brother and I were fascinated by the ice house as it was so deep. And we both loved the big Wellingtonia—its bark was so soft that you could dig your fingers into it.

Q. Did Thicket have any ghosts, or secret tunnels?
A. Yes! There was talk of a 'grey lady' and a little boy dressed in old-fashioned clothing. And I remember my mother telling me about the sound of carriage wheels on the gravel approaching the front door. But when the servants went to see who it was, there were no carriages at all! In the old days the carriages used to drive across the park as there was a lodge on the Wheldrake Road where they would turn in. I remember the ruts in the park made by the wheels. There was also talk of a tunnel, going from Thicket to the rectory at Wheldrake.

Q. When did you leave Thicket and go to Thorganby Hall?
A. We left before it was sold and 1952 is the year that comes to mind.

Q. What was Thorganby Hall like?
A. Very nice but of course much smaller than Thicket. We kept our ponies in a field next to the hall. It had a small garden at the front and a larger one at the rear. It had stables, garages and a dovecote. My mother loved fantail pigeons and I remember them very well. Mac our chauffeur came with us from Thicket and he had a flat on the premises. We stayed at Thorganby Hall until around 1962 when we left to go to York to live at 129 The Mount, which none of us really liked as we didn't like living in York and missed the country. After that we moved to Deighton House where we were very happy until my father's death in 1979 after which my mother moved to a cottage in Escrick. I lived and worked overseas for 22 years from 1967, and I used to come home from time to time and it was mostly to Deighton House or Rectory Cottage in Escrick.

Social Changes

The problems with finding new tenants for the farms of the Thicket Priory Estate and finding domestic staff have been mentioned previously. The upheavals of the two World Wars, combined with alternative work such as factory, retail and clerical employment for women, saw a huge fall in the numbers of residential servants. The end was in sight as the few domestic servants that were still available were increasingly unwilling to 'live in'. Incomes for large estates had fallen dramatically, due to these factors, and it was perhaps in response to this that the Dunnington-Jefferson family sought new ways of monetising their assets.

In April 1951 Sir John and Lady Dunnington-Jefferson opened the gardens of Thicket Priory to visitors, on Saturdays and Sundays, 2pm to 7pm, at a charge of one shilling. Perhaps a decision had already been made, as two months later the announcement was made in the press that the priory, with its fifteen acres of land and two-acre lake was for sale, Sir John and Lady Dunnington-Jefferson and their two children intending to live in Thorganby Hall. However, a buyer could not be found.

In April 1953 St. Helen's Church in Thorganby was in urgent need of restoration, requiring £2,300. The villagers had managed to raise (over three years) £1,500 towards the cost. In response, Sir John and Lady Dunnington-Jefferson again decided to open the gardens at Thicket Priory and also part of the house to visitors. The gardens were in full bloom with daffodils, bouquets of which were on sale together with a country produce stall; and in the house Sir John had provided access to his collection of Flemish and Dutch paintings. The open day at Thicket managed to raise £190 towards the church restoration fund.

The Return of the Nuns

Eventually, in 1954, a buyer was found for Thicket Priory: Carmelite nuns who needed a new home from their site in Exmouth. The Prioress, Mother Mary of Saint-John Vavasour, came from Yorkshire—her family home had been Hazlewood Castle. She felt drawn to relocate the community to the north of England. The sale was subject to vacant possession, so in May 1954 the entire contents of Thicket Priory were put up for auction:

> By order of Lieut.-Colonel Sir John
> Dunnington-Jefferson, D.S.O.
> THICKET PRIORY, THORGANBY, YORK
> HENRY SPENCER and SONS will sell by
> Auction in A MARQUEE ON THE PREMISES
> on THURSDAY and FRIDAY, MAY 27 and 28.
> A LARGE PORTION OF THE
> **CONTENTS of the HALL**
> including EXCELLENT PURNITURE.
> A cut glass Chandelier with 12 scrolled branches for electric candles, English, Continental and Oriental decorative Porcelain, including a Crown Derby Dinner Service (138 pieces), fine Dessert Services, a Worcester Barr, Flight and Barr Tea Service, items of Davenport, Leeds, Sevres, Minton, Capo-di-Monte, Staffordshire, Delft and Chinese Porcelain, Silver and Plate, Carpeting and Rugs, Venetian and English Table Glass, Curtains, Linen, the Library of Books, Oil Paintings by or attributed to Melchior, Hondecooter, Peter Wouvermans, John Wycke, John Molenaer, L. Hubner, Sir Godfrey Kneller, Pictures of the Dutch and Italian Schools, Naval Prints, Colour Prints and Engravings, an Armstrong-Siddeley Atlanta Saloon Car, 1937 model, Kitchen and Outside Effects and Miscellanea.
> Sale to commence at 11.30 a.m. promptly each day
> VIEW DAY SATURDAY, MAY 22,
> from 10.30 a.m until 5 p.m. by illustrated catalogue only (2s. each) which admits two persons.
> Also ON VIEW on the MORNING OF SALE.
> Light refreshments at reasonable charges.
> HENRY SPENCER and SONS, Auctioneers.

Following the removal of the contents of Thicket Priory, the Carmelites began moving into their new home during the latter half of 1955, the conveyance being completed on 12 December of that year. The story of the move to Thicket is told in the book *Countryside & Cloister: Reminiscences of a Carmelite Nun* by Marie T. Litchfield.

Remarkably, after almost eight centuries, nuns were once again resident in Thicket Priory, just yards away from the site of the original priory.

Following the sale of Thicket Priory, Sir John and his family moved into Thorganby Hall. Later, in 1958, Sir John was honoured once more, when the queen signified her intention of conferring a baronetcy in her Birthday Honours, 'For public services in Yorkshire', which was duly gazetted in the *Supplement to The London Gazette* of Tuesday, 3rd June, 1958, page 3511.

Mr. Smith, the estate manager, continued to manage the estate farms and lands until the 1964, when Sir John sold the remainder of the estate, comprising 3,080 acres in Thorganby and West Cottingwith, to John Bealby Eastwood, thus ending the long and distinguished tenure of the Dunnington-Jefferson family.

Plan of the Thicket Prior Estate prior to the sale in 1964

Subsequent Ownership and Thicket Priory IV

The Thicket Community, c. 1975

In 2005 the Carmelite nuns celebrated their 50 years at Thicket Priory III and a plaque to mark the event was commissioned and installed, but unfortunately it was broken when an attempt was made to take it down in preparation to move it to a new home.

However, it became clear to the nuns that the maintenance of such a large house was untenable and simply too big for their needs. In January 2006 they decided to move to a smaller and more practical monastery, suitable for their requirements. Thicket Priory III and a part of the surrounding land was sold as a private residence, and the nuns then commissioned the building of a new priory on the land they had retained, within the walls of what had been the Victorian kitchen garden—used as such when Sir John and his family lived at the priory—closer to the site of the original Thicket Priory. This included the burial ground of the original medieval nuns.

The planning application for this new monastery, which I will now refer to as Thicket Priory IV, gained widespread support from the local surrounding villages who wished the nuns to stay as 'a praying presence'. Planning permission was granted in December 2007 and the sale of Thicket Priory III could then be completed. The new owner, Bruce Corrie, agreed not to take physical possession, in order that the nuns could continue living at Thicket Priory until they built their new monastery and could take up residence.

Building work on the new monastery then began in early 2008 with the construction of a new driveway to the site, and the cordoning off of the original Cistercian burial ground. The construction of the main building commenced in June 2008. The site manager was Dave Taylor, and together with Mary of Carmel they attended all the site meetings between the architects and contractors, having been involved throughout the planning and building process. All the nuns walked to the site each Sunday to view the progress and would often have a meal close to the kitchen garden. During the digging of the foundations an old well was discovered, and this was restored and preserved.

The new building was designed for a community of fifteen and research showed that the original Cistercian foundation had space for fifteen choir nuns. In January 2009 a service was held for the blessing and rededication of the 'new' bell before being set in place above the new chapel. The bell actually dated from

1640 and was kindly donated by the neighbouring Anglican parish of Saint Helen, Wheldrake, and several parishioners attended the rededication service, with the bell being renamed 'Joseph'.

The work on the monastery slowed during the frosty winter months, but restarted in earnest in the spring. Four stained glass windows had been designed by a local glazier, Joseph Burton, for the chapel at Thicket Priory III in 1997, and these were removed and installed in the new chapel.

Carmelite Monastery, Thicket Priory

In the Easter of 2009 a large congregation attended the Vigil in the new chapel, including many of the Anglican friends and people who had worked on the building. The landscaping and internal fittings of the new monastery were then completed and the official handover from the construction company, Hobson and Porter of Hull, to the Carmelites took place 18 May 2009. The nuns were then able to move into their new purpose-built monastery which took place three days later.

Epilogue

Thicket Priory was founded during the reign of Henry II for a small cell of Benedictine nuns and was one of the humblest, if not the humblest, of nunneries which sprung up in Yorkshire during the twelfth century. Initially built of wood, and thatched, it eventually acquired walls of stone, glazed windows and a leaded tiled roof and was described as such when it was eventually dissolved by Henry VIII during his infamous Dissolution of the Monasteries, in the late 1530s. Thicket Priory was one of the last to be dissolved, which occurred in 1539.

Although the priory was destroyed the accompanying farm buildings were retained, and when the site of the priory was exchanged by the king in 1542 to John Aske for various manors held by Aske in Sussex, it continued as a substantial farm estate. Aske eventually sold the estate to John Robinson, a prosperous merchant of London, who then left it in his will to his son, Henry Robinson, who later sold the estate to his brother Humphrey Robinson.

Humphrey Robinson decided to make the estate his home and had a substantial house built there around 1622, initially referred to as Thicket Hall, but which eventually gave way to the name Thicket Priory, and the Thicket Priory Estate was then born.

The estate passed to the Jefferson family in 1803 and descended by the will of Robert Jefferson to a cousin, John Dunnington, in 1812, but conditional upon John Dunnington adopting the name of Jefferson.

In 1844 the Rev. Joseph Dunnington-Jefferson decided to have a grand new residence built to replace the old Thicket Priory (Thicket Hall) of the Robinson family, and embarked on an ambitious building project — a new Thicket Priory. The architect he employed for this prestigious project was none other than Edward Blore, notable for his works on Lambeth Palace, Buckingham Palace, Hampton Court Palace, Windsor Castle, and many others.

The Dunnington-Jefferson family moved into their new grand Thicket Priory III in 1848 and the former Thicket Priory (Thicket Hall) then fell into decay. It was during the tenure of Thicket Priory III that the estate reached its pinnacle of success, followed by its lowest ebb, brought on by two world wars and the introduction of onerous estate duties.

In 1954 Sir John Dunnington-Jefferson sold Thicket Priory (but not the estate) to a community of Carmelite nuns.

After almost eight centuries, nuns were once again resident in Thicket Priory, just yards away from the site of the original priory.

Colin Blanshard Withers